Christianity and Politics

Christianity and Politics

The Attempted Seduction of the Bride of Christ

Christopher R. Petruzzi

RESOURCE *Publications* • Eugene, Oregon

CHRISTIANITY AND POLITICS
The Attempted Seduction of the Bride of Christ

Copyright © 2013 Christopher R. Petruzzi. All rights reserved. Except for brief quotations in critical publications or reviews, no part of this book may be reproduced in any manner without prior written permission from the publisher. Write: Permissions, Wipf and Stock Publishers, 199 W. 8th Ave., Suite 3, Eugene, OR 97401.

Resource Publications
An Imprint of Wipf and Stock Publishers
199 W. 8th Ave., Suite 3
Eugene, OR 97401
www.wipfandstock.com

ISBN 13: 978-1-62032-652-7
Manufactured in the U.S.A.

All scripture quotations, unless otherwise indicated, are taken from the Holy Bible, New International Version®, NIV®. Copyright ©1973, 1978, 1984 by Biblica, Inc.™ Used by permission of Zondervan. All rights reserved worldwide.

Contents

Preface vii

1. The Unholy Alliances of Politics 1
2. A Selective History of Christians in Politics 11
3. The Economics of Politics 44
4. The Nature of Politics 53
5. The Way of the World 66
6. Taxation and the Redistribution of Wealth 75
7. How to Change Behavior 81
8. The Civil Rights of Christians 97
9. The Christian's Wealth 102
10. Israel and Foreign Policy 112
11. Preparation for the End Times 137

Conclusion 159
Bibliography 163

Preface

I WAS RAISED AS a member of the Presbyterian Church USA in Peoria, Illinois, but did not learn the Gospel message or have the experience of accepting Jesus as my Savior until the age of 39 in California in the spring of 1991. I thank Allen Heneveld who played an important role in leading me to the Lord and Jim Hayman whose Bible studies through a student club at California State University Fullerton (CSUF) where I am a tenured professor played an important role in my training. These thanks should not be interpreted as meaning that either of those brothers in Christ agrees with or takes responsibility for anything I have written in this book. I would also like to thank my most significant undergraduate economics professor from Wabash College, the late Ben Rogge, and my graduate professor, Art Laffer. Their influence is apparent in parts of this book, particularly that of Laffer in the chapter on Redistribution of Wealth. I began writing this book in 1995 when I was on a paid leave from my duties as a professor. Most of the book was finished by 1998, and I sent it to twenty-eight Christian publishers, all of whom rejected it. In the year 2000 Paloma Partners asked me to manage a hedge fund using fully automated trading, and that activity kept me busy for most of the next decade. After closing that fund with an excellent rate of return to the investors, I returned to teach at CSUF and took another leave during 2010–2012. During this period, I made some minor changes in the book and submitted it to Wipf and Stock which accepted it for publication. While many of the references in the book are from the late 1990s, I do not believe that the importance of any of those has been reduced by events of the last fourteen years.

My theology in this book is based on the assumption that the entire Bible is true and that Christians should follow all of the instructions in the New Testament at their face meaning. This assumption implies that no part of the Bible contradicts any other part, and thereby provides a means of interpreting some verses correctly by taking the meaning which

Preface

does not contradict any other verse. This theology implies that Christians should follow Christ's instructions given in the Sermon on the Mount.

I am aware that many contemporary Christians do not believe that the Sermon on the Mount and some other parts of Jesus' sayings are intended for modern Christians to follow. In part, those Christians base their interpretation on the fact that Jesus' instructions to His disciples in Luke 10:4 were changed in Luke 22:35–36. I believe, however, that Luke 22:37 explains those special instructions as applying only to the period immediately before Jesus' arrest. That is the only interpretation which I am able to make which follows my assumption that the Bible is consistent, and I do not believe that this one passage would provide instructions to Christians which are inconsistent with much of the rest of the New Testament and that it would do so without an explanation anywhere in the New Testament. Nonetheless, it is possible that I am wrong in this, and either way I hope to have and to show no less love for Christians who make contrary interpretations.

I offer my apologies to my children, Lillian Caroline Petruzzi and Vivian Audrey Petruzzi, for the time that work on this book has kept me from them. All things, including this book, are dedicated to Our Lord, Jesus Christ, but in thanks for the support she has shown, the mortal to whom this book should be dedicated is my wife, Georgina Sailer Petruzzi.

1

The Unholy Alliances of Politics

"Let us rejoice and be glad and give the glory to Him, for the marriage of the Lamb has come and His bride has made herself ready." (Rev 19:7)

THE BRIDE OF CHRIST is the Church, the body of all Christian believers. As His Bride, our souls should be preoccupied with serving Him. When the world takes us away from Christ's methods, we lose our focus on Christ, and in this way we are seduced. The result of the seduction is that we are yoked with people, causes, and methods which are not holy. Throughout history some Christians have yielded to the seduction of politics, and history shows that this was a loss for Christianity. Today, Christians are again encouraged to become actively involved in politics. I hope to show through this book that when Christians use the ways of the world to become involved with politics it is an unholy alliance that does not serve God.

The term "politics" has several meanings. In this discussion I will use the definition which states that politics is the struggle for the control of government. It is the conflict between different individuals who seek to change legislation and policy so that the legislation and policies follow what they want as opposed to what other people want. As such, politics has winners and losers.

The administration of government does not fall under this definition of politics. Daniel served as an administrator for Babylonian kings Nebuchadnezzar and Belzhazzar before serving the Mede king, Darius. While he held fast to his beliefs, he did not try to influence government policies in a way which had winners and losers. Similarly, Joseph, the son of Jacob, served the Pharaoh of Egypt by giving advice and administering public works, but he did not engage in politics. Conflicts and outcomes which have perceived winners and losers are at the core of politics, but mere administration does not fall into those categories.

Early Christians like Paul used the Roman judicial system to protect their rights to witness for Christ, and this was not engagement in politics either. Courts in Rome (and in the United States today) do not make new laws or new policies. They only interpret existing laws and apply that interpretation to specific situations. That is not politics, and it is appropriate for Christians to peaceably use the judicial system to protect their own rights. My chapter entitled The Economics of Politics will explain this in more detail,

Because of the State's exclusive right to use violence to enforce political outcomes, political conflicts are intense. As Mao-Tse tung stated in his "Little Red Book," "Political power rolls out of the barrel of a gun."

The purpose of this book is to analyze the appropriate participation of Christians in these conflicts, with particular emphasis on politics in the United States. I believe in the truth of the Scriptures, and I assume that the reader has those same beliefs. Therefore, while this book uses some analytical techniques of economics and philosophy, my arguments are all consistent with the best interpretations of Scripture which I am able to make.

It is sometimes argued that Christians should be involved in politics because if good people do not take roles of political leadership, then those positions will be taken only by bad people. This argument misses both the meaning of Christianity and the purpose of politics. Christians are not good people, for there are no good people. Christians are sinners who have been forgiven and filled with the Holy Spirit. We are part of God's Kingdom, not the Kingdom of this World. We do not need and should not want to use worldly methods to compete with worldly people to run the affairs of the world. In fact, this book will show that worldly methods of politics are not productive activities for Christians.

The argument concerning good people also misses the purpose and nature of politics, and the analysis of that purpose and nature is the principal theoretical development in this book. I first show that Christian political activity has been unsuccessful throughout history. It damaged the souls of Christians and hindered the salvation of others. I then proceed to develop an exposition of the nature of politics. I show in this exposition that the nature of politics is selfish activity in which one party prevails at the expense of others. I proceed to look at specific ways that Christians sometimes seek to use politics to further their own ends, and show that Christians can always serve Christ better without using the ways of the world to influence politics. While most of this discussion is theoretical, I also discuss some specific issues (such as abortion) which are of interest to many Christians.

Despite the fact that worldly involvement in politics is not the best way to serve Christ, some Christian issues may also be political issues. Some of Paul's letters to Christians dealt with order in society and the treatment of various classes of people. These inherently political issues are also Christian issues. In the US, the Christian charity which we show for others is politicized through tax deductions, matching grants, and government supported welfare. By contrast, Christian charity is penalized or even prohibited in some oppressive Third World dictatorships. Part of our Christian respect for human life is enforced by government (as in laws prohibiting murder) while parts are ignored (by allowing abortion, for example). Even Christian prayer and worship are affected by politics.

Writing in The Political Meaning of Christianity,[1] Glenn Tinder states that it is desirable that Christians have an influence on political issues. I do not know of any Christians who contest that point. The issue is one of how Christians influence political issues. The worldly way of influencing those issues is to join in the political struggle through electoral politics and, sometimes, through the violent means of war and revolution. Peter tried the worldly method of influencing politics when he cut off the ear of the high priest's servant. He was rebuked by Jesus for doing this. Except for this instance, no Christian in the New Testament tried to use worldly means to influence politics. Christians are exhorted to pray, witness, give to charity, and to be good examples, and the position of this book is that these Christian activities should be the exclusive means by which Christians work to exert influence on the political process.

Christians in the United States sometimes look to the Constitution for guidance on the appropriate political activity of Christians. Some Christians also look to other writings of Thomas Jefferson and George Washington to see if those political leaders ever intended a complete separation of church and State. Those efforts miss the pertinent point for Christians. Christian behavior is not necessarily what the nation's Founding Fathers wanted and

---

1. Glenn Tinder, The Political Meaning of Christianity (Baton Rouge: Louisiana State University Press, 1989).

what is revealed in their writing. It is what God wants and reveals in the Bible. While we must comply with every law that is not opposed to God, the fact that political participation by Christian groups may be legal does not imply that it is holy.

Jesus said that his Kingdom was not a kingdom of this world. Despite the allegations of the Pharisees, Jesus was not trying to take Caesar's place. While Jesus was still on earth, the disciples apparently wanted him to establish a worldly government with himself as king. When the disciples were filled with the Holy Spirit on the Day of Pentecost, however, they acquired a better understanding of Christ's Kingdom and no longer sought a worldly government. Instead, Paul and the other authors of the New Testament told Christians to submit to the world's government, to honor the worldly king, and to pray for him. The influence of the apostles on the government came from evangelism, prayer, charity, their own good examples, and preaching about the Scriptures. While Paul repeatedly used the Roman courts to enforce his right to preach, his use of courts was consistent with obedience to the existing state since the courts only applied the state's laws.

Proponents of Christian participation in politics often associate themselves with "traditional values" or "family values," but because Christianity is not worldly, Christian values are not traditional values and they are not family values. As Jesus said, " For I have come to turn a man against his father, a daughter against her mother, a daughter-in-law against her mother-in-law. A man's enemies will be the members of his own household" (Mt 10:35–36).[2] Jesus also tells us not to follow the traditions of men. St. Paul states, "For though we live in the world, we do not wage war as the world does." Consequently, we should not try to accomplish our Christian goals through the worldly method of politics. While Christians have an advantage over non-believers in Godly activities such as prayer and being good examples, we are at a disadvantage in worldly methods. The early American religious leader Roger Williams had a good understanding of this principal when he taught that the characteristics for success in government were not the characteristics for success in religion, and we should be grateful that his teachings had an important influence on the authors of the U.S. Constitution. (The Godless Constitution, Isaac Kramnick, WW Norton and Company 1997)[3] The kingdoms of the world belong to Satan, and their ownership (in exchange for worship) was rejected by Jesus Christ

---

2. All Bible quotes in this text are from the New American Standard Bible (NASB).
3. Isaac Kramnick, The Godless Constitution WW Norton & Co., 1997).

The Unholy Alliances of Politics

(Luke 4:6). When we seek those Kingdoms of the world for ourselves, we fail to walk in Christ's holy path.

Four recent Presidents of the United States have indicated that they were evangelical Christians: Richard Nixon, Jimmy Carter, William Clinton, and George W. Bush. The history of their administrations should provide some lesson to Christians; a born-again Christian who lives in the world of politics is a fish out of water (see note 1). By trying to use the ways of the world to accomplish Christian goals, he divides himself and, in the end, fails. No amount of intelligence, training, and hard work will let the Christian succeed in a world which belongs to Satan.

Christians are called to be peacemakers and to be meek. We are to love our neighbors as we love ourselves. We are not to seek the things of this world (Mt 6:19). Whatever we ask in the name of our Savior Jesus Christ will be granted. We are told to change the world by evangelism (Mark 16:15) and by our example (1 Tim 4:12).

Christians sometimes reject a sole reliance on the biblical tools of prayer, charity, evangelism and example out of perceived practicality. Their argument seems apparent. If we could effect change by ourselves in other ways, wouldn't God want us to do so? Should Christians just sit back while worldly people rule the world? Wouldn't it be better if Christians ruled the world instead? After all, the Bible says that Christians are to someday rule the world. Shouldn't we try whatever means are available to bring Christian practices into our society today?

While well-intentioned, it is obvious that the rationale of practicality is secular and non-biblical. Practicality can be a disguise for worldliness, and the nature of practical politics is quite worldly. In fact, the essence of politics is un-Christian worldliness. The argument of practicality misses the major message from both the Old and New Testaments: that the way of man does not work while faith in God does. The Bible gives us alternatives of prayer, charity and evangelism, and these methods have proven to be successful for Christians.

Humanism is the philosophy which is concerned with the achievements of man as opposed to the ways of God. Christians who attempt to change the world through their own efforts in worldly politics are therefore humanists. They are trusting the efforts and ways of man rather than using the ways of God and waiting for God to act. Since born-again Christians are filled with the Holy Spirit of God, their attempts to use the ways of man make them a house divided against itself, and for that reason they must fail.

Christianity and Politics

Although Christian pacifism goes hand-in-hand with refusal to participate in worldly politics, this is not a book on pacifism. Many books have already been written on that subject, and I believe that a Christian should only need to read Christ's Sermon on the Mount, particularly Mt 5:38–48 to be convinced that Christians are not to be violent. These verses are well-known, even to unbelievers, and we make ourselves poor witnesses for our faith when we resist with violence. The atheist philosopher Bertrand Russell entitled his best known work Why I am Not a Christian.[4] In that book Russell wrote that many contemporary politicians claimed to be Christian, but he doubted if they would pass the test of not hitting back if he struck one on the cheek. When Christians strike back, every unbeliever knows that we have failed our faith.

(see note 2).

At the same time, the New Testament describes many interactions of Christians and the government. Paul pleaded his case in the courts and sought to convert political leaders. He sought the protection of police from the mob, and demanded that his rights as a Roman citizen be respected. While the actual meeting is not described in the Bible, it is generally believed that Paul was called to bring his case to the emperor in Rome, and that he appeared before the Emperor Nero, who then had him beheaded. The Bible and secular history both teach that Christians were persecuted for their beliefs and practices, but they persisted in the face of this persecution. Christians are called on to obey laws which do not prohibit the practice of their faith and to show respect for governing authorities. God even gave instructions for ruling Israel, and some Christians believe that the Body of Christ is the modern Israel.

I hope in this book to leave the reader with a better understanding of the Christian's appropriate position with respect to government. In order to acquire a good perspective on that position, it is helpful to begin with our history.

Note 1: Richard M. Nixon was a member of the Society of Friends ("Quakers"), while James Earl Carter was a Southern Baptist and a self-declared born-again-Christian. Clinton was also a Southern Baptist and at the time of his graduation from high school he was so committed to Christ that his speech as valedictorian was a call for salvation and discipleship. According to The Washington Post[5] George W. Bush was among the most

---

4. Bertrand Russell, Why I Am Not A Christian (Touchstone, 1967).
5. The Washington Post, Sep 16, 2004, A01.

The Unholy Alliances of Politics

openly religious presidents of all time. He prayed daily and regularly turned to the Bible for guidance. Only God knows which of these men really had a personal relationship with Jesus Christ, but all four professed to be Christians. In general, however, fundamentalist Christians who have been born again do not have high opinions of the work of the first three of these presidents, and the fourth is so disliked around the world that his presidency continues to be a source of international ill will.

Nixon expanded an unpopular war and, following a resolution of impeachment which was introduced in the U.S. Senate, he resigned with the disgrace of criminal charges. While few people discuss the issue, Nixon also bears some disrepute from having campaigned as a conservative but having acted as the most politically left-wing president of the twentieth century. Nixon recognized Red China (thereby ending diplomatic relations with Taiwan). He increased taxes and generally expanded the federal government. In one day (August 15, 1971) Nixon put a freeze on all wages and prices, took the U.S. off the gold standard which had prevailed for the previous 100 years, and increased import duties by the largest percentage in U.S. history. Through that one presidential order alone Nixon did more to increase the control of the federal government over the U.S. economy than Lyndon Johnson did during his entire presidency. Taking the U.S. off the gold standard is the probable cause for the U.S. CPI increasing by about 300 percent during the 1970s and may be the principle factor behind problems in worldwide financial markets which continue into the twenty-first century.

While less dramatic, Carter was a similar failure. On the domestic side, the Carter administration expanded the federal bureaucracy, gave us more taxes and higher inflation, and produced the worst U.S. economic statistics since the Great Depression. On the international side, the U.S. appeared to be on the path to becoming a second-rate power and completely failed a well-publicized attempt to free our own diplomats being held hostage in the Iranian embassy.

Born-again Christians tend to have their lowest opinions reserved for Clinton, and his administration will probably be best remembered for blatant dishonesty and the most sordid sexual scandals to ever disgrace the White House. While strongly identifying himself as a Christian, George W. Bush was responsible for the unprovoked invasions of Iraq and Afghanistan. As a consequence of those invasions, it is difficult for missionaries outside of the U.S. to represent Christianity as a religion of peace. George

W. Bush is also blamed by many people around the world for the severe economic downtown which followed his administration.

By contrast, many fundamentalist Christians believe that the best U.S. president in the twentieth century was Ronald Reagan. Reagan was a divorced actor who married a divorced actress. While William Clinton and George W. Bush were regularly photographed in church on Sundays holding their Bibles, Reagan is said to have attended church services on only three Sundays during his eight years in the White House. While Nixon, Carter, and Clinton were regarded even by their detractors as exceptionally bright men with great understanding of the workings of government, Reagan fell asleep during meetings with cabinet secretaries and was sometimes unable to differentiate factual history from the plots of movies. Nonetheless, the Reagan administration produced spectacular success in both international and domestic affairs. To a large extent, the prosperity of the U.S. in the last part of the twentieth century is due to the tax cuts and deregulation which Reagan initiated.

Note 2: Unfortunately, few Christians are brave enough to advocate pacifism. I recently heard one of California's best-known born-again pastors on a radio program in which a listener asked for his interpretation of Luke 22:36–38 where Jesus tells his disciples to "let him who has no sword sell his robe and buy one." This is the only verse in the New Testament which can be construed to mean that Christians should ever behave violently. (While Revelations deals with the Beast's war against the saints, Rev 13:10 states, "If anyone kills with the sword, with the sword he must be killed. Here are the perseverance and the faith of the saints," indicating that even in this war the appropriate Christian defense is through faith, not a sword.) The pastor's interpretation of Luke 22:36–38 was that while Christians are generally called to be peacemakers, "we should not be stupid." If someone threatens our families, he said, we should defend ourselves. He noted that Christians had a tradition of doing this in war. That pastor's message seems to have the implication that Christ's Sermon on the Mount told us to do something "stupid." No part of the Bible contradicts any other part, and Christ's words in Luke 22 were certainly not contradicting the Sermon on the Mount and the many verses which clearly say we should not behave violently. The term "sword" in Luke 22 is sometimes interpreted to mean Scriptures since Ephesians 6:17 refers to "the sword of the Spirit, which is the word of God." Since Christ prophecies his arrest in Luke 22:37, another interpretation is that this was a command for the disciples to follow only prior to Christ's arrest in Gethsemane. When the disciples produced two swords Christ said, "It is enough" (Luke 22:38). Peter's use of one sword to cut the ear of the high priest's servant played an important role when Jesus rebuked him and healed the servant.

While I believe that the pastor on the radio was incorrect on his interpretation of Luke 22:36, he was sadly correct on the Christian tradition. The European wars of the past thousand years have been predominantly ones where Christians killed other Christians. Christ's entire Sermon on the Mount seems stupid to the world, but it is infinite wisdom to those who know him. As Paul states in 2 Cor 10:3–4, "For though we walk in the flesh, we do not war according to the flesh, for the weapons of our warfare are not of the flesh, but divinely powerful for the destruction of fortresses." The fact that Christians appear to the world to be fools is one of the messages of the New Testament.

The whole morality of war is un-Christian, but it protects the Christian. Most soldiers believe that it is moral to kill other soldiers, but that civilians should not be attacked. This is an un-Christian morality, since we have no reason to believe that it is any less of a sin to kill a soldier than to kill a civilian. Most soldiers are drafted, and even among the "volunteers," few are knowledgeable, willing participants. During the 1991 Gulf War with Iraq, that country drafted males as young as 14 years. The penalty for refusal to fight was that the non-participant and that person's entire family were put to death. Is there any way to hold the 14-year-old responsible for his participation under those circumstances? Even in wars without a draft, the issues are so complex and the propaganda so intense that each participant believes himself to be on the side which serves God. That has been the case in every modern European war that I have studied.

The principal issues to the Christian should be salvation and service to Christ. If enemy soldiers have not been saved through knowing Jesus Christ as their Lord, then we are preventing their salvation by killing them. That would only leave the "saved," and it is clear that Christ does not want his brethren to fight each other.

The fact that soldiers generally do not attack civilians serves to protect Christian pacifists. From the perspective of a soldier, the Christian pacifist is not a threat. His labor and earthly goods can be used by the victorious army. As long as our attacks are spiritual, we are not waging war in the same dimension as earthly kings and princes. As stated in Romans (13:3), "For rulers are not a cause of fear for good behavior, but for evil. Do you want to have no fear of authority? Do what is good, and you will have praise from the same."

I recently saw a man wearing a tee shirt in which the front said "the meek shall inherit the earth." The back of the tee shirt said "Yeah right" and showed the face of a fierce looking football player along with the symbol of a popular maker of athletic shoes (Nike). The tee shirt was clearly mocking the Sermon on the Mount, and that is understandable since the message that the meek shall inherit the earth is one which makes no sense to worldly people. That same message is an article of faith for Christians. Its truth must be an integral part of our lives.

2

A Selective History of Christians in Politics

"... how he made war and how he reigned, behold, they are written in the Book of the Chronicles of the Kings of Israel." (similar to several verses in 1 Kings and 2 Kings)

CHRISTIAN PARTICIPATION IN POLITICS is not a mere analytical problem in which history is irrelevant. Academic researchers who analyze disagreements with colleagues in subject areas which seem theoretical often find that their disagreements over theory are based on each individual's different observations of past data. To some extent theological differences among Christians also have historical sources. Consequently, an accurate understanding of history can help Christians to reach a correct understanding of their own faith.

There are numerous books on the history of Christianity, but many of the older works do not use a standard of reliability acceptable to modern researchers. In past ages, accuracy and reliability were not accorded the high level of importance which they are given today. This, along with the fact that authors frequently had religious, political, and economic incentives to distort the truth means that recent histories written by contemporary academics are often more accurate than histories written only a few generations after events took place. While we accept the truth of the Bible regardless of documentation, we should require documentation of any mortal source. It is with this standard in mind that I am writing this short history of Christians in politics.

The modern historian attempts to give accuracy to his work by using, whenever possible, contemporaneously written accounts of first-hand eyewitnesses who had no incentives to distort the truth. While this degree of rigor is rare in pre-modern works, it is amazingly evident in one ancient source. The New Testament of the Bible is almost entirely composed of eyewitness accounts and contemporaneous letters! Since Paul and ten of the disciples were ultimately executed for their refusal to recant their testimonies of Jesus, the New Testament represents a standard of truth which is not only acceptable to a modern historian but which would even be admissible as evidence in a court of law. Recent discoveries of ancient documents which were contemporaneous with the disciples indicate that the New Testament has not had any meaningful changes since the original version, just as the Dead Sea Scrolls showed that parts of the Old Testament have been the same since ancient times. (Of course, it has been revealed to many believers, including myself, that the Bible is actually true, but the fact that most of it meets modern standards of evidence is a point which may be used to convince unbelievers.) (see note 1)

Since the events described in the New Testament end in the First Century AD, we cannot rely on the Bible for history after that period. Subsequent pre-modern works of Christian history were generally written by clergy who were not trained to do discerning, accurate research, and who had strong incentives to write histories which glorified the leaders of their respective sects and the political leaders who supported those sects. The descriptions of a domestic king were likely to be unfavorable only if the king's dynasty was usurped or, like John, the brother of Richard the Lion Hearted, he had attempted to reduce the power of the clergy. An unsuccessful claimant to the throne (like William the Conqueror's son Stephen) is labeled a usurper by contemporaneous historians even if contemporaneous law may have made the claim legitimate (through the lack of precedent within England for primogeniture in this case). Otherwise the contemporaneous historian would meet the same oppression (usually death) which was accorded the unsuccessful claimant.

The same principle applied in reverse when the contemporaneous historian had incentives to glorify a leader. Hence, even though Richard the Lion Hearted impoverished England by undertaking an unsuccessful foreign war and had to be ransomed from his own allies, his support of the clergy brought glowing descriptions from the contemporary historians (who themselves were clergy). In the United States, similar situations made it almost impossible for authors to write anything which did not glorify the stories of the political leaders such as Founding Fathers and President

A Selective History of Christians in Politics

Abraham Lincoln. In either case, it was considered treasonous for anyone to make critical statements, and some dissenters were hanged for treason after both the American Revolution and the Civil War. While many Christians have been willing to suffer martyrdom for Christ, few secular historians have been willing to suffer martyrdom for the sake of historical accuracy. Part of the job of the modern historian, therefore, is to discern which past statements are factual and which were altered by politics.[1]

While histories written with political motives are often unreliable, Christians know that the truth sets us free (John 8:32). We must pursue Truth whatever the consequences to our worldly icons. To do otherwise would be a violation of our Christian ethic.

This is a selective history of Christians and politics since I am only writing about the historical involvements with politics which I most often hear cited by other Christians as a justification for current political activity by the Church. While this lets me avoid discussion of the generally recognized sordidness of periods such as the Spanish Inquisition and Henry VIII's foundation of the Church of England, I still describe many unpleasant facts. Fortunately, this unpleasantness is overshadowed by the glorifying story of the Church in its early years of martyrdom.

When researchers who have been exposed to different facts develop different theories it is lamentable but understandable. When researchers who have different theories describe the same facts differently, however, it makes the reader suspect their integrity. With the foreknowledge that the reader may be suspicious of my portrayal of facts, I have tried to be as fair as possible in my interpretations. In this chapter on history, I have tried to use original sources of contemporary eyewitnesses and unbiased records or secondary sources which have good citations of the original. I have also tried

---

1. Unfortunately, even the accuracy of some modern works is hindered by their authors' biases. In Bertrand Russell's *Why I am Not a Christian* he states that "millions of unfortunate women were burned as witches" by Christians. Of course, it is unChristian to burn anyone, but a gross exaggeration leads to distortion in viewpoints. According to Will Durant's *History of Civilization* the greatest persecution of witches was in Germany in the sixteenth and seventeenth centuries, where about 3,000 were burned or otherwise executed. The total number executed in the British Isles was less than 2,000, and Italy and Spain only executed about a dozen accused witches between them, as their inquisitions focused on other heresies. In all, it is unlikely that more than 10,000 people have been executed as accused witches. Despite the facts that Russell's allegation was incorrect by more than a factor of one hundred and that his writing made the basic error of failing to separate Christianity from the behavior of self-proclaimed Christians, Russell was given the Nobel Prize in literature for *Why I am Not a Christian*.

to cite all of my references to factual statements which may be controversial, and if the reader knows of reliable sources which contradict these facts, I ask you to send me your information so that I can improve future work. To the best of my research abilities, however, all that I am writing is true.

The Early Church: Constantine and the Martyrs

The martyrdom of early saints is widely known, in part due to the work of John Foxe who began writing his manuscript entitled *Actes and Monuments* which is popularly known as *Foxes Book of Martyrs* in the early 1550s (Zondervan, 1978) Like most writers of his time, however, Foxe was probably more concerned with story than with accuracy. There are no references listed in his work even though the events he describes took place prior to his birth. It appears to me and other modern readers of this work that parts of the *Book of Martyrs* are inaccurate. I have every reason to believe that those inaccuracies were unintended, but I have relied on other, better documented sources for my facts. My principal source for this section is W.H. C. Frend's *Martyrdom and Persecution in the Early Church*[2] but the only important difference with Foxe is explained in my text, so that the reader who trusts Foxe has no reason to suspect my own presentation. I cite Frend as the source of my information even where Frend himself cites an earlier source.

Beginning with the stoning of Stephen, there were several waves of persecution against Christians in the early church. Foxe and Frend both describe ten waves of persecution, and some Christians believed that these ten waves had been foretold in metaphor by the ten plagues in Egypt and the ten horns of the Beast in Revelations. For the most part, these persecutions were based on the Roman law which required that everyone burn incense before a statue of the emperor. Prior to the reign of Emperor Nero, Jews were exempted from this requirement, and Christians were exempted *de facto* since they were generally considered a Jewish sect. Even into the second century AD, classical historians make many references to Judaism but few to Christianity.

Nero's persecution increased in 64 AD (probably only four years after Paul's arrival in Rome) with the burning of the city which he blamed on Christians. Christianity itself was made a capital crime, punishable by crucifixion, being fed to beasts, or other tortures for all Christians except for

---

2. WHC Frend, *Martyrdom and Persecution in the Early Church* (Lutterworth Press, 2008).

Roman citizens (like Paul), who had the right to the less painful execution of being beheaded.

After Nero's death in 68 AD, historians are unclear whether Christianity remained illegal or if continued persecution by authorities was simply allowed out of tradition. Either way, persecution was only sporadic. For the most part, Roman officials took a liberal attitude toward Christianity and saw no reason to punish a sect which abided by all Roman laws, except for the worship of the emperor and, among some, participation in military service. Still Christians kept to themselves. Tertullian (circa 160–230 AD), regarded as the founder of the Latin Church, said "Nothing is more foreign to us than the state. One state we know--the universe."[3] Tertullian's followers believed, however, that no man need obey an unjust law, and while they would not fight for the empire, they would pray for it.

Despite the tolerance of public officials, Christians were unpopular among the pagan subjects of the Roman Empire. Ancient Romans were generally devout in their worship of pagan gods, and the Christians' refusal to worship the official gods was seen by some pagans as a sign of atheism. They were also considered strange. Even in the middle of the second century, many Christians followed some Mosaic rules of diet, and blood was apparently drained from animals before the meat was eaten. Their similarity to Jews brought them much of the resentment which the public held in reaction to the Jewish rebellions which took place in Israel over the years AD 68–70, 115–116, and 132.

Early Christians were unworldly. Tertullian was so opposed to material wealth that he said "Even to become a tailor was dangerous since it was to transform God's sheep into costly raiment."[4] Some Christians were so convinced of the imminence of Christ's return that they would not even plant fruit trees, believing that there was not enough time left for the trees to mature. When, as a result of public demand, Christians were martyred in Lyons and Vienne in 177 AD, the Christians were so humble that while they still lived they refused to call themselves martyrs. They considered themselves unworthy of the title accorded to Christ. They had a complete absence of the fear of death by martyrdom.

Further persecutions took place sporadically over the next 134 years. Carthaginians persecuted the local Christians in 203, but subsequently Christianity apparently grew at a rapid rate in Carthage. Even though

3. Frend, 272.
4. Frend, 273.

Christianity and Politics

Saturn had been the leading god of Carthage and the Berbers, no dedications to Saturn can be found after 272 AD in Africa. Apparently, by that date, Christianity had replaced paganism in Carthage.[5] At the same time, some Christians had become more worldly. In 272 AD Bishop Paul was the chief financial minister for Queen Zenobia in Antioch and he lived "like a lord."[6]

In 255 AD the Goths invaded the Roman city of Pontus, and Christians were reported to be openly disloyal to Rome, even sharing in the Goth's loot. This produced increased apprehension by the Roman government, and in 257 AD the Emperor Valerian renewed active persecution of Christians. Under Valerian's reign, one only had to admit being a Christian to be put to death. Still, official records show that many Christians openly professed their faith. The trial of Fructuosus, the Bishop of Tarragona was as reported follows:

> Proconsul: Are you the bishop?
> Fructuosus: I am.
> Proconsul: You were.
> (After which the proconsul had Fructuosus burned to death.)

Despite this harsh persecution, Eusibius reports that Christians voluntarily made the journey to Ceasarea in order to confess their Christianity before the governor and to become martyrs.[7]

In June of 260AD, Valerian was defeated in battle and taken captive. In 261 AD Valerian's son, the Emperor Gallenius published an edict of toleration under which Christians were permitted to worship unmolested. Nonetheless, Eusebius (260?–340?) reported continuing persecution, leaving Frend to suggest that Gallenius' edict was only an unenforced political concession made to the growing Christian populations of Rome and Alexandria.[8]

In 282 AD, following an anarchical period of 35 years in which 37 different men were proclaimed Roman Emperor, the Empire began a system of shared rule. Diocletian took the title of Caesar as the defender of the East and his co-ruler, Maximian, who was also titled Caesar, became the defender of the West. Each Caesar appointed a successor, who received the

---

5. Ibid., 335.
6. Ibid., 330
7. Ibid., 321.
8. Ibid., 326

A Selective History of Christians in Politics

title of "Augustus." Diocletian's successor was Galerius while the Western Augustus was Constantius Chlorus, the father of the future Emperor, Constantine, and the husband of Maximian's step-daughter.

Despite the shared rule, the Empire itself was not divided under the new order, and laws were enacted in the names of all four Caesars and Augusti. Galerius saw Christianity as the last obstacle to absolute rule,[9] and in February of 303 AD, all four rulers decreed a new persecution calling for the death of Christians attending Christian assemblies. The persecution continued for eight years and resulted in the deaths of about 1500 Christians, in addition to the non-fatal punishment of many more. The edict was enforced vigilantly in the East, and two Christians who were among the emperor's senior officials at Nicomedia were martyred in 303.[10] In Britain and Gaul, where Constantius was in charge, however, enforcement of the edict was limited to burning a few church buildings.

By 311 AD, it was apparent that the persecution of Christians was unsuccessful. Durant states "the sight or report of heroic fidelity under torture strengthened the faith of the wavering and won new support for the hunted congregations." It was impossible to destroy Christianity when the death of each martyr resulted in several new converts. Just before Galerius' death in 311 AD, he initiated an edict of toleration, recognizing Christianity as a lawful religion and asking, in return, for the prayers of Christians. Despite Galerius' edict, local persecution of Christians continued.[11]

In 305 AD, Diocletian and Maximian abdicated in favor of their Augusti, Galerius and Constantius. When Constantius died the next year, his son, Constantine, was proclaimed emperor by the Gallic troops. Too distant to intervene, Gallerius affirmed Constantine as Caesar. Meanwhile Maximian's son, Maxentius was proclaimed emperor by the Praetorian Guard in Rome. When Maximian returned to political life by attempting to replace Constantine as commander of the Gallic troops in 310, he was defeated. Constantine crossed the Alps, and, in a decisive battle in 312 AD at the Mulvian Bridge, nine miles north of Rome, he defeated Maxentius. Constantine proceeded to conquer the rest of the Empire and to make himself its sole ruler.

The battle at the Mulvian Bridge was a milestone for Christian involvement in government, since it is generally associated with Constantine's

---

9. Durant 651 (see p.20).
10. Frend, 331.
11. Ibid., 386.

conversion. The sincerity of Constantine's alleged conversion, however, is one of the great questions of Christian history. Constantine attributed his victory at the Mulvian Bridge to the help of a deity, but he did not openly embrace Christianity and state that the deity was Christian until twelve years later in 324 AD. The Roman arch commemorating his victory does not name the deity, and it was presumed by the Roman Senate to be a pagan god. While he stated that he saw a flaming cross in the sky prior to his victory, the cross was not the cross of crucifixion, but the symbol which Roman Catholics know as the laborum. Followers of the pagan god Mithras were the leading opponents of Christians at that time, and the laborum is very similar to the Mithraic cross.

Constantine's coins had pagan inscriptions until 323 AD. Like previous emperors he held the title of pontifex maximus (taken later by Popes in the Roman Catholic church), indicating the leadership of the pagan cult which had originated in Babylon a thousand years earlier, and he carried out the position's traditional ceremonial tasks. He restored pagan temples, ordered the taking of omens before new ventures, and used both pagan and Christian rites in dedicating Constantinople. He used pagan magic formulas to protect crops and cure diseases. December 25 had been recognized by Romans as the date of the birth of Mithras (Durant) and had previously been recognized by Babylonians as the birth date of their principal god, Nimrod (Hislop). Constantine declared that the celebrations on December 25 would continue as the birth date of Christ. Suspecting their political opposition, Constantine put to death both his son and his wife in 326 AD. He chose not to be baptized until he was on his deathbed.

Evidence that Constantine was Christian includes that Constantine gave Christian bishops the authority of judges, exempted the church from taxation, and gave the churches the property of intestate martyrs. In 312 AD he provided freedom of choice in religion for Christians and pagans alike. His mother was a Christian, and Constantine gave his sons Christian educations. He participated in Christian philanthropy. He said that he was a Christian.

Constantine's conversion may have been only a shrewd political maneuver to gain the support of Christians who by this time were a majority. It could also have been sincere, and it is not my place to judge that Constantine was or was not a Christian. Until Christ returns, that could only be known with certainty by God. Constantine professed that his conversion came as the result of a sign from God, so I suggest that we follow I

A Selective History of Christians in Politics

Thessalonians 5:20–21, and not despise prophetic utterances, but examine everything carefully, holding fast to that which is good.

Quantitative Analysis

The numbers of Christians and martyrs during the period of Roman persecution lend themselves to an interesting analysis. First, there is the question of the number of Christians in the Roman Empire at the time of Constantine's alleged conversion in 312 AD. Some historians refer to Christians around that time as a minority while Eusibius (Bishop of Caesarea, circa 260–340AD) reports that Christians were in the majority throughout the Empire by 311 AD.[12] Of course, part of the problem is that the distribution of Christians was not homogenous. It appears that Christians were a higher percentage of the population in Gaul, Northern Africa and the East than in the rest of the Empire.

Another part of the problem with estimating the number of Christians is that the number was growing. The Book of Acts tells us that on the day of Pentecost (33 AD) about 3,000 souls were added to the number of believers. As an approximation let us say that the number of believers in 33AD was 3500. The population of the Roman Empire in 312 AD is estimated by most historians to have been around 100,000,000. Therefore, if Christians were a majority there were at least 50,000,000 Christians in 312 AD, and I will use that figure as the high estimate of the number of Christians. Since, even if the Christians were a minority, they were a significant minority, I will use 12,500,000 as the low estimate of the number of Christians in 312 AD. This means that, at the slowest, the number of Christians doubled on average every 23.75 years, and, at the quickest, the number of Christians doubled on average every 19 years. These figures explain how historians looking at data from the late third century would state that Christians were only an important minority while historians looking at data from 312 AD would state that Christians were a majority. A persistent growth in Christianity is consistent with the fact that in 260AD Dionysus of Alexandria had reported that some areas of the countryside had not even heard of Christianity but by 311AD Christianity was known throughout the Roman Empire.[13] The high rate of growth means that if the growth rate were constant, Christians might have been only 15 percent of the population in 274 AD, and yet they still might

12. Ibid., 335.
13. Ibid., 336.

have been 60 percent of the population in 312 AD. It means that the highest estimates (which are also the latest) are probably the most accurate indication of the number of Christians in 312 AD.

While the growth rate in the number is interesting because it is high from a perspective of long periods of time, it is also interesting because it is low from a perspective of short periods of time. Modern Christians often think of the Early Church as a period of explosive growth which cannot be matched today. Even at the highest estimate of growth, however, the number of Christians only doubled every 19 years. This means that if each committed Christian led one other person to the Lord every nineteen years, and introduced one extra convert during his lifetime, and if the new believers had the same commitment, then the growth in the number of committed Christians would match the growth in the Early Church. While it would not be easy, and not every committed believer would be able to make the goal, an average of one new committed believer every nineteen years does not seem to be an unattainable evangelical success.

Another interesting analysis concerns the number of martyrs in the Early Church. According to Frend, the total number of martyrs who were put to death between 33AD and 312 AD is between 3000 and 3500. Foxe's Book of Martyrs describes a Roman legion from Thebes which was composed entirely of Christians, and which was martyred in 286 AD, but this is omitted from Frend's estimate of the number of martyrs. Frend states that there are no credible contemporaneous sources for the story of the martyred legion, and the accounts contain contradictions. He therefore doubts that the story is true.[14] Even if we include this legion, however, the total number of martyrs rises to about 10,000. To make a very high, but not totally unreasonable estimate of the total number of Christian martyrs put to death between 33AD and 312 AD let's say that the number was 20,000. While every Christian martyr is important, this number is interesting because it is so low. Many battles with only 20,000 deaths are so unimportant that they are not even recorded in history. In the five-day 1991 Gulf War the estimates of Iraqi casualties were generally over 100,000 and most observers rounded their estimates to the nearest 10,000.

While the number of Christian martyrs was tiny compared to deaths in military conflicts, their impact was enormous. Most military conflicts accomplish nothing. For the most part, fifty years after the conflict ends, national borders are exactly where they started, and there is no change in

14. Ibid., 360.

international relations. Yet millions of men march off to battle and die for these wars. On the other hand, a few thousand Christian martyrs turned the world on its end. For most of these martyrs, they would only have had to throw some incense on the fire before the statue of the Roman Emperor, and they would have been released. Instead, they chose to let their Roman guards put them to death. The power of this testimony was so great that many prison guards converted to Christianity on the spot.

The power of martyrdom is consistent with Scriptures. 1 John 5:4 "For whatever is born of God overcomes the world; and this is the victory that has overcome the world, our faith." Even the anti-Christian philosopher Nietzsche said "The mightiest men have always bowed reverently before the saint, as the enigma of self-subjugation and utter voluntary privation. They (the mightiest men) learned to have a new fear before them; they divined a new power, a strange, still unconquered enemy."[15]

It is impossible to defeat Christian martyrs when their very deaths increase the number of believers. The Roman ruler Galerius admitted this defeat when he ended the prohibitions against Christianity in 311 AD. A few thousand Christian martyrs succeeded where no foreign army had been able. Those Christians never sought political power; they only sought the things of Heaven. When they gave their lives for Heavenly things, the empires of this world fell before them.

B. Charlemagne and the Containment of Islam

As already noted, Christianity was the predominant religion throughout the Mediterranean world by 312AD. This predominance became regionally divided with the rise of Islam.

Mohammed was born in Arabia in 570 AD and lived until 632. He was the author of the Koran which partially is founded in the scriptures of the Old and New Testaments. Under the Koran, Muslims (those who submit to God) believe in one God, Allah, whose identity is said to be the same as Yahweh (Jehovah) who is worshipped by Christians and Jews alike. (Some historical sources state that the name of Allah came from a pagan deity. I will discuss this possibility in the chapter on Israel.) Muslims believe that Jesus was the greatest prophet, but not the Son of God, and that Jesus did not die as an atonement for sins. Instead, Jesus escaped the crucifixion, and each individual must atone for his own sins by doing sufficient good deeds

---

15. Friedrich Nietzsche, *Beyond Good and Evil* (Dover Publications 1998), 51.

to outweigh his sins on God's scales. They believe that Jesus was God's messenger bearing instructions on living a religious life, while Mohammed (the Seal of the Prophets) completed the message by adding new revelations and the instructions for a worldly kingdom. They also believe that the Koran corrects the Bible which misquotes Jesus and the other Prophets.

Mohammed converted the polytheistic Arabians and founded the secular government which Muslims regard as God's authority on earth. While the Koran instructs Muslims to never be the aggressor in war, Mohammed expanded his government by military power. After several military defeats, Mohammed ultimately led his own armies to victory. During the century following Mohammed's death, his followers established Islamic governments throughout most of the Mediterranean region.

There is a belief popular among Christians that Muslims forced conversion at the point of a sword or killed those whom they conquered, but that is not shown by historical records of the period before the Crusades, nor is it condoned by the Koran. Before the Crusades, most Islamic governments allowed freedom of religion, and there were 11,000 Christian churches in Islam in the early Ninth Century. Broadbent notes that Syrian Christians were prominent in the Islamic court at Baghdad in the ninth century (*The Pilgrim Church* p. 70). Most Muslims followed the proclamation of Abu Bekr (the first caliph and Mohammed's father-in-law) "Molest not the religious persons who have retired from the world, but compel the rest of mankind to become Moslems or to pay us tribute."[16] In keeping with this, the principal penalty on Christian laity was first a land tax and later a poll tax to which Moslems were exempt.[17] Persecutions of Christians under Moslem rule took place, but persecution was not the general rule. Caliph al-Hakim burned churches and synagogues around the year 1000, but he later relented and rebuilt the destroyed shrines.[18]

When Kalid conquered Egypt in 641 AD, he proclaimed freedom of worship and was welcomed by Monophysite Christians.[19] In 744 AD, however, 24,000 Christians in Egypt converted to avoid the poll tax.[20] Despite this tax, some Christians stayed in their faith, and there are Christians throughout the Islamic world. About 5 million Coptic Christians remain

16. Durant 188, 218 (see p. 20).
17. Hoyt, Europe in the Middle Ages, 118.
18. Durant 285.
19. Ibid., 282.
20. Ibid., 289.

A Selective History of Christians in Politics

in Egypt, and about 5 percent of the population of Iraq publicly identify themselves as Christian.[21] In 712, Moors (followed by Arabs) invaded Spain and gave it religious freedom. Most of the Christians in Spain subsequently converted to Islam.

Military limits to the Islamic expansion were first made when Charles Martel and his son, Pepin the Short, defeated the Moslems in 732 at Tours. Charles Martel was the illegitimate son of Pepin II, who defeated his siblings in battle to become the mayor of the palace and Duke of Austrasia. Charles Martel was a nominal Christian who supported Boniface and other missionaries, but also confiscated church lands and sold bishoprics to his generals. When a monk protested his use of church property, he had the monk beheaded. His son, Pepin the Short, had more harmonious relations with the church, having rescued the papacy from Lombard kings and given it land through the Donation of Pepin. In return, Pope Stephen II made Pepin "king by the grace of God" and declared that no one except Pepin's descendants should ever be King of France. The defense of Gaul (France) against the Muslims appears to have been motivated by the desire to save this earthly kingdom as opposed to the desire to save souls.

Pepin the Short's son and heir was Charlemagne. With Muslims at his borders and polytheistic pagans within Gaul, his military successes were mostly against non-Christians. In the late 700's he beheaded 4500 Saxons who chose death rather than baptism. Charlemagne's campaigns were not entirely motivated by the love of Christianity, however, since he and his Moslem allies attacked the Christian town of Pamplona in 777.[22] Charlemagne had four successive wives and five concubines. Nevertheless, the Roman Catholic Church declared him a saint in 1165.

Analysis of the Islamic Containment

The Islamic expansion before the time of Charlemagne is one of the great enigmas of church history. Unlike the military conquest's of the Ottoman Turks almost 1000 years later, the early Islamic expansion was not marked by forced conversions to the Islamic faith, yet most Christians in the conquered areas chose to convert. In the early 300's Christians adhered to their faith so strongly that they would rather be tortured to death than to merely throw incense to the statue of the Emperor. The faith of those

21. James and Marti Hefley, Arabs, Christians, and Jews (Hannibal Books, 1978). .
22. Durant, 462..

martyrs defeated the world. Less than 400 years later, the descendants of these same Christians freely converted to Islam with little pressure other than the incentive of a tax break.

Part of the answer to this enigma is that Islam had beliefs related to the Christian Bible.

Muslims regard both Christians and Jews as "people of the Book" who worship the same God and who should be treated with respect not due to pagans. Islam did not deny Jesus' existence, but stated that Jesus was the greatest of the prophets. These similarities may have made Islam more palatable to Christians who then chose to convert.

While these similarities may have made conversion to Islam more palatable than conversion to Emperor worship, they are insufficient to explain the conversion of true Christian believers. Christianity is based on a personal relationship with God through His only begotten Son, Jesus Christ, and the fact that Christ died in full penitence for our sins. Islam teaches none of these beliefs, and this repudiation of the core of Christianity would make it impossible for any true Christian believer to accept Islam.

The secularization of Christianity and its corruption by Church leaders stand out as plausible reasons for the Islamic success in producing voluntary conversions. Beginning in 324 AD, most Christians accepted the leadership of the secular/pagan pontifex maximus who also took the title of Pope. Their personal relationship with God was replaced by a system in which a priest was the self-proclaimed intermediary. Direct reading and interpretation of scriptures was discouraged by the Church. Hence, by the time of Mohammed, many people who called themselves Christians did not have a personal relationship with God and had little understanding of what Christianity was all about. Christianity most likely was perceived by most to be a religious system of priests, cathedrals, and transfers of wealth. Kings and nobles legitimized their positions with church rites, and in return they supported the church.

Based on this perspective, the success of Islam was not a defeat for Christianity. It was simply the substitution of one state religion for another. Pepin the Short, Charles Martel, and Charlemagne were mainly concerned with preserving their own political dynasties which used the state religion called Christianity to provide legitimacy. When similar political dynasties fell to the military power of Islamic invaders, their state religions collapsed and Islam filled the void. That is why few people needed to be forced to convert to Islam. The great population of true Christian believers which existed at the time of Constantine had already died out and had not been replaced with new believers. Islam found an empty house which had been swept clean and was waiting for a new occupant (Matthew 12:44).

C. The Crusades

When I state to Christians that no military conflict can be holy, the response I hear most often involves the Crusades. The image which many Christians seem to have of these conflicts comes less likely from a history book than from Cecil B. DeMille's film which exalted the Crusaders as Spirit-led saints. Unfortunately, an accurate historical account of the Crusades presents a story which brings shame on the names of Christians.

Prior to 1070 AD, Jerusalem was occupied by the Islamic Fatimids who institutionalized religious liberty for Christians and even helped with the building of Christian churches. This changed, however, when the Seljuq Turks captured Jerusalem and began persecuting Christians. The persecution continued until the Fatimids recaptured the city in 1098 and renewed religious freedom for the Christians.

The First Crusade began in 1095 AD with speeches by Pope Urban II calling for "vengeance" against "a wicked race." The Byzantine Empire had lost ground to the Seljuq Turks and Urban's speeches were at least partially prompted by the request for aid from Emperor Alexius I in Constantinople. At the same time that Byzantium was losing ground to the Turks, Western Christians were expanding the areas under their influence by the taking of Sicily from Muslims in 1091 and the partial reclamation of Spain in 1085. Urban's cooperation with his theological rivals in Constantinople may have been further encouraged by Italian merchants who wanted to extend their control of the Mediterranean to the East. A total of over 30,000 men responded to the call. "The first victims were not Moslems, however, but the Jews of Eastern Europe, whose communities were devastated as the would-be Crusaders made their way east and south towards Constantinople and the Holy Land."[23]

Only 12,000 Crusaders made it to the gates of Jerusalem in June 1099, the majority having died or retreated on the journey through Muslim territory. By this time, the Fatimids who had no history of persecution against Christians had re-conquered Jerusalem, and the Seljuq Turks

---

23. Roberta Harris, *The World of the Bible*, (London: Thames and Hudson, 1995), 176.

Christianity and Politics

who persecuted Christians had been expelled, thereby making the official reasons for the Crusade moot. Nonetheless, the Crusaders besieged Jerusalem, gaining victory after 40 days. (Modern historians attribute the military success of the First Crusade to the fact that Europeans had begun to use stirrups on their horses, making their cavalry more powerful than that of the unstirruped Muslims.) The Christian priest Raymond of Agiles reported the conquest as "wonderful" with "Saracens tortured for days and then burned in flames" Men, women, and children were hacked to death by the Crusaders, who did not take the trouble to distinguish between the Muslim, Jewish and Christian citizens of Jerusalem. It was a scene of rape and pillage with about 70,000 Muslims massacred. Most of the Jews were taken to the synagogue where they were burned alive, and babies were flung over the city walls. Eastern Orthodox, Armenian, Coptic and other Christians were slaughtered. (*Arabs, Christians, and Jews*, James and Marti Hefley, Hannibal Books 1978) One Crusader eye-witness account of the aftermath of the battle takes an astonishing delight in the scene of carnage, "In all the . . . streets and squares of the city mounds of heads, hands and feet were to be seen. People were walking quite openly over dead men and horses . . . what an apt punishment."[24]

The level of brutality with which the Crusaders treated the people of Jerusalem was extraordinary and in total contrast to the clemency which had been shown by the Muslim Caliph Omar when he conquered the city in 638 and by Saladin when he re-took Jerusalem in 1187. In both cases the behavior of the Muslims was more Christ-like than the behavior of the Christians.

The Second Crusade began in 1146 AD as a response to Muslims re-taking many cities (but not Jerusalem) which had been conquered during the First Crusade. Although initially large in number, the Christian armies were routed and destroyed by Muslims (who by this time had learned to use stirrups) with no significant victories for the Christians.

Saladin's re-taking of Jerusalem was the impetus for the Third Crusade which began in 1189. While the Third Crusade was initiated by Frederick Barbarossa (who had been ex-communicated by the Pope), it was principally lead by Richard I (Lion Hearted), the Norman King of England. Following brutal battles in which the Christians, and then the Muslims executed their prisoners, King Richard proposed ending the conflict by marrying his sister to Saladin's brother. The proposal was rejected by both Saladin

---

24. Roberta Harris, *The World of the Bible*, (London: Thames and Hudson, 1995), 176.

A Selective History of Christians in Politics

and the Church in Rome. Fighting continued but a truce was negotiated under which Saladin agreed to grant pilgrims free passage to Jerusalem and to give Italians control of certain port cities.

During Richard's journey back to England he was captured by the nominally Christian Duke Leopold of Austria. Leopold turned Richard over to the Holy Roman Emperor, Henry VI, who demanded that England pay ransom of 150,000 marks or roughly twice the annual revenue of the English crown. Richard's fellow Crusader, Phillip Augustus of France, used Richard's absence as an opportunity to seize Richard's property in France, and bribed the Emperor to keep Richard longer. Four years after his release and subsequent return to England, Richard was killed in a siege against one of his own vassals.

The Fourth Crusade was probably the greatest embarrassment to Christians. While organized with the stated intention of re-taking Jerusalem, the Crusaders began by taking the Christian city of Zara from Hungary against the direct orders of the Pope. They proceeded to conquer the Christian city of Constantinople, also against the direct orders of the Pope. The Crusaders sacked the city, robbing homes, shops, and churches. They raped the women, including Greek Orthodox nuns, destroyed manuscripts and works of art, and carried the best of Constantinople's gold and other treasures back to Venice. They established a French speaking government in Constantinople. After the sacking of Constantinople, most of the Crusaders returned home with their loot. Some of the plunder from this Crusade (almost entirely against other Christians) sits in Venice today. The Venetians consider this treasure a trophy, but sincere Christians must think of it as a stark reminder of the hollow rewards of sin. All of the participants in this Crusade were ex-communicated from the Roman Catholic Church.

The Fifth Crusade, begun in 1217, was another attempt to re-take Jerusalem. The Crusaders experienced early success against the Egyptian city of Damietta and were offered the surrender of most of Jerusalem, the return of Christian prisoners and the return of the True Cross (presumably the wooden beams upon which Christ was crucified). They refused this offer, however, and proceeded to fight and lose a war with the Muslims. As part of the truce, they were given the True Cross (but not Jerusalem). While some claimed the True Cross as a victory, it seems highly unlikely that the actual cross upon which Jesus had been crucified was preserved, discovered, and correctly identified. This is just as well, since our faith is based on our relationship with God and not on any relics.

Christianity and Politics

The Sixth Crusade was initiated in 1228 by Frederick II, the son of Barbarossa, who had also been ex-communicated by the Pope. Frederick negotiated a peace with the leader of the Saracen army, al-Kamil, under which the Crusaders received Nazareth, Bethlehem, and all of Jerusalem except for the enclosure of the Dome of the Rock, which was considered a holy site by the Moslems. The pact was denounced by the Pope as an unholy compromise. In 1244, the Christian rulers of Jerusalem made an alliance with the Moslem ruler of Damascus against the Egyptian sultan. This alliance proved unfortunate, since later that same year the Egyptian sultan captured Jerusalem, plundering the city and killing many of the inhabitants.

The Seventh and Eighth Crusades were organized by Louis IX of France and took place between 1248 and 1271. For a short time, the soldiers of the Seventh Crusade re-took Jerusalem, but it was soon reclaimed by the Muslims. The Seventh Crusade ended with Louis being captured by the Muslims and held for an enormous ransom. Following his return to France, Louis returned to Tunisia for the Eighth Crusade, and he died there "of a flux" in 1270. This final crusade ended a year later with no victories.

In the year 1212, there were two children's crusades. The first was led by a German boy named Nicholas, and it ended when Nicholas and the 30,000 children who followed him could not find ship owners to take them to the Holy Land. The other children's crusade was lead by a 12 year old French boy, Stephen, who said that Christ had appeared to him while he was leading a flock of sheep. Ship owners out of the French port of Marseille offered to take Stephen and his followers to Palestine at no charge, presumably out of Christian charity. Instead, they tricked the children. Of the seven ships of children which left, two sank and the passengers of the other five were sold into slavery in Tunisia and Egypt by the ship owners. Frederick II tracked down the ship owners and had them all hanged.

Analysis of the Crusades

It is not always possible to discern motivations from actions, and not all Crusaders had the same motives. Nonetheless, it appears from the history of the Crusades that the principal motives of the Crusades' leaders were not Christian. The apparent motives of the Crusades' leaders were political and economic. The Northmen who ruled most of Europe were expanding their frontiers at the same time as the Muslims were pushing to the West. A confrontation was inevitable. At the same time, Italian merchants were

A Selective History of Christians in Politics

competing with the Muslims for the control of Mediterranean shipping, so there was an economic incentive for the invasion.

The Crusades' leaders encouraged their subjects to enlist in the armies with every means at their disposal. Racial hatred for the darker skinned Saracens, stories of injustice, and the prospect of loot were all part of the motivation. The worst part of the motivation, however, was placing religious importance on obtaining possession of the True Cross and political control of Jerusalem. These last motivations were the most damaging because they may have had appeal to sincere Christians and corrupted their spirituality with false values. They substituted the idolatry of created things for men's relationship with God.

The Crusades increased the power of the Papacy and of religious orders such as the Knights Templar. Venice and Genoa benefited from expanded shipping routes. The Church began the sale of indulgences to raise money for the Crusades, and that practice remained, probably hastening the reformation. Some Asian technology and culture was brought back to Europe.

Overall, the Crusades probably did more harm to Christianity than any other episode of history. Prior to the Crusades, Islamic governments and peoples generally showed the toleration of Christians which Mohammed asked of his followers. The brutal and unfair treatment by the Crusaders produced a fear and intolerance which has persisted. "The Moslem powers, once tolerant of religious diversity had been made intolerant by attack." (Durant p. 609)

As a direct result of the Crusades, it is more difficult today for Christians to witness to Muslims than to any other religious group. The salvation of over a billion souls who are living today in countries with Islamic governments is hindered by these acts that are nine hundred years old. This is the terrible legacy of the Crusades. In the end, the Crusaders traded millions of souls for pieces of wood and a few cold metal objects which still sit untouched in a Venetian vault.

The Crusades established a pattern for the future political participation of Christians. The pattern is as follows: worldly leaders seeking personal economic gains represented the political means to their economic ends as a Christian cause. Christians pursued the cause, thereby substituting the idolatry of the political end for their relationship with God. Of course, the political solutions required that other parties lose at least as much as the worldly leaders would gain. In the end the worldly leaders may or may not have succeeded, but the souls of Christians were damaged.

The damage of the Crusades to the salvation of Muslims was dramatic and it continues into the modern world. Billy Graham is well-known for his evangelistic Crusades to lead people to Christ, and will typically lead hundreds of new souls to make a decision for Christ at his rallies. A few years ago one of Billy Graham's associates led a series of evangelistic services in Beirut, but only one decision for Christ was recorded. Local observers attributed the relative failure to the animosity which remains in the Middle East for any program that is called a Crusade.[25] Groups such as Harvest Crusade and Campus Crusade for Christ should seriously consider substituting the word "mission" or another word for "Crusade" in order to not harden the hearts of the large portion of the world's unbelievers who are Muslim.

D. The Puritans

The Puritan government in England is one of the saddest examples of what happens when Christians are seduced by politics. By all accounts, the Puritans were sincere Christians. They emphasized man's spiritual relationship with God rather than religious ritual. Using modern terminology we would say that they were born-again fundamentalists. Their example is also one of the most important episodes of Christians in politics since it has similarities to the situation of Christians in the United States today.

The Puritans began in the 1500s as a group of Bible-believers who were probably influenced by Calvin, John Knox, and Wyclif. They were first called "Puritans" around 1564 as a term of derision due to the fact that they demanded purification of English Protestantism from all forms of worship and faith not found in the New Testament. In the 1570s, under the influence of Thomas Cartwright and Walter Travers, the Puritans developed a concept of the Church under which Church leaders would have the power to enforce an outward observance of Godly living by threatening violators with penalties of excommunication and death. They advocated popular election of Church leaders, thereby becoming a threat to the monarchy which held powers of appointment to Church office. In the 1580's some former Puritans (the Separatists) began to leave the Church of England to form their own groups of worship. While the majority of Puritans remained

---

25. Hefley, 106 (see p. 36).

A Selective History of Christians in Politics

with the Church of England, others left their assemblies to join the Baptists, the Quakers, the Independents who sought their own republic, and the Millenarians who expected Christ's eminent return and replacement of the monarchy with Divine government. Each of these groups was considered heretical by the Puritans.

The Puritan venture into politics began with the Parliamentary elections of 1586 where the Puritans campaigned against candidates who were not sympathetic to their cause. Their pamphlets questioning the authority of the Queen's bishops resulted in the hanging of two Puritan leaders in 1593. In 1604, the new king, James I, attempted to reconcile the Puritans with the rest of the Church of England, but enforced punishment on everyone who did not comply with his proposed compromise. Part of the compromise was that James I agreed to the Puritan proposal for a new translation of the Bible, which became the King James Authorized Version.

Despite the compromise, Puritan pamphleteering continued, and Puritan influence on Parliament grew. By the 1620's Parliament was in fairly open opposition to the King, imprisoning his Chancellor, Francis Bacon, in 1621. When Parliament banned him for life from politics, Bacon retired to philosophy and developed the modern scientific method. (After the Restoration, the Royalists returned the favor to literature by sending John Milton to prison, thereby enabling him to focus on *Paradise Lost*.)

By 1625 approximately three quarters of the House of Commons was Puritan. In 1628 Parliament severely restricted the taxation powers of King Charles I and attempted to reform the practices of the Church of England. In 1629 the King ordered Parliament to adjourn, and when it refused, he sent troops to dismiss the Members.

In order to raise funds against an impending rebellion by Scotland, Charles reconvened Parliament in 1640. When Parliament instead chose to ally with the Scottish rebels, Charles again dismissed the Parliament. The Scots then defeated England and took possession of Northern England, so Charles again reconvened Parliament to raise funds for the reparations demanded by Scotland. Instead, Parliament proposed to take control of the military, and the King charged its leaders with treason. The result was the Civil Wars of 1642–1646 and 1648–1649.

Oliver Cromwell became the Puritans' commanding general and so inspired his troops with the righteousness and godliness of their cause that his New Model Army was never defeated, even when they faced armies twice their numbers. The Puritan troops prayed before each battle, used clean language, and studied the Bible in their free time. King Charles was captured and, facing imminent execution, showed the fortitude of turning down Parliament's offer of a pardon in return for concessions which the king viewed to violate his duties to the Church of England. He was beheaded in 1649.

Following King Charles' execution, many Englishmen viewed him as a martyr, and a book containing the late King's personal notes and reflections sold out thirty-six editions within a year. The Puritan Parliament quickly responded with laws of censure against all unfavorable publications and speeches.

Cromwell led the new government. His first task was the invasion of Ireland, which had agreed to support a restoration of the monarchy. Cromwell's armies were successful. He began with the policy of massacre against the towns which resisted him. While Cromwell's successor generals were less brutal, Sir William Petty estimated that out of a population of 1,466,000 which lived in Ireland in 1641, approximately 616,000 perished from the war, plague and starvation by 1652. Catholicism was outlawed, and to even harbor a priest was made punishable by death. The children of Catholics were taken from their parents to receive training in Protestant homes, attendance was required at Sunday Protestant services, and 2.5 million acres of Irish land were transferred from Irish Catholics to Englishmen and their Irish supporters.

The Puritans next military venture was against Scotland. While the Scots had previously been the Puritans' allies, the Puritans had eliminated all the Presbyterians from Parliament with Pride's Purge, and the Scots viewed this as a violation. Scotland allied with Charles II who agreed to establish Presbyterian Protestantism in all his dominions and his personal household. Again, Cromwell's armies were undefeated, and Scotland was made subject to England. Cromwell also waged war against the (Protestant) Dutch and allied with (Catholic) France to wage war with Spain. To finance these wars, Parliament levied exorbitant taxes and sold most of the King's lands, all of the properties of the Anglican Church, the estates of many royalists, and about half of Ireland.

In England, the Puritan Parliament confiscated two thirds of the property of all Catholics (about a quarter of the population at that time) and offered rewards for the apprehension of Catholic priests. When in 1653 the 56 Members of the Parliament of 1640 who survived the war and purges (out of over 500 elected) were about to make themselves England's permanent lawmakers, Cromwell entered with his soldiers, called some Members "drunkards" and "whoremasters" and disbanded the Parliament. Cromwell created a new Parliament composed of men chosen by his military leaders from Puritan congregations and proposed a reign of saints under the presidency of Jesus Christ.[26] Following much debate, this new parliament was so divided on religious questions that it voted for its own dissolution. After considering the title of "King," Cromwell was declared "Lord Protector" by his army.

The Puritan government suspended virtually all civil rights. Puritans believed in infant baptism, and in 1648 they imposed life imprisonment on everyone who opposed it.[27] This was repealed in stages in 1653 and in 1654 when they sought the support of Baptists whom they invited, along with Presbyterians, into their government. Quakers were imprisoned until 1657 when Cromwell released them with instructions to justices that the Quakers be regarded as deluded persons. (In America, the Puritans continued to hang Quakers for preaching. The last such executions took place in Boston in 1692.)

Puritans understood the history of Christmas as a pagan holiday, and therefore the celebration of Christmas was permitted only by fasting and atonement. No work, sports, or other non-religious activities were allowed on Sundays. Everyone was required to fast from meat on Wednesdays. Divorce was allowed, but adultery was made a capital crime.

Oliver Cromwell died of a fever in 1658, after naming his son, Richard, as his successor. Richard resigned less than a year later and retired to private life in France where he lived under the pseudonym of "John Clarke" to avoid the notoriety of the name Cromwell. Parliament and the army contested each other for power, but by this time the English people were not willing to support either. Crowds openly asked for the return of the monarchy. Facing revolt, in 1660 Parliament sent 50,000 pounds to Charles II with the request that he return to assume the power of King as his birthright. Charles complied, thereby ending England's Puritan government.

Analysis

There is little doubt but that many of Puritans were committed Christians who were led by the Bible. By all accounts Oliver Cromwell was a sincere

---

26. David Hume, *History of England IV* (Philadelphia: Porter & Coates, 1870), 550.
27. Durant VII 214. Firth, 149. JJB Bury, *History of Freedom of Thought*, 86

and devout Christian who prayed at every occasion. He was also one of the most brutal men in history.

Puritan government was an unequivocal failure. Retention of power required major compromises with the Baptists and Presbyterians, but Parliament still begged for the King's return only 11 years after they had beheaded his father. Cromwell's military success is sometimes cited as evidence that God was on the side of the Puritans. God ordains all events of history, but if we believe that Cromwell's military success indicates the correctness of his faith, then we must say the same for Genghis Khan and many other pagans. A better explanation is that Puritan troops exhibited the same bravery as the Muslims who believed that their death on the battlefield guaranteed them a life in Paradise.

The Puritans left us with a legacy that acts as a barrier to the salvation of their own descendants and the groups they persecuted. Few modern Believers belong to denominations with Puritan origins, and both England and New England are filled with apostasy. So many Irish died from the military conflict or from the starvation which followed their dispossession of the land that virtually every Irishman had close relatives who died at the Puritans' hands. It is no coincidence that, outside of the Islamic world, Ireland is probably one of the most difficult nations for Protestant witnessing. Violent struggles for the control of Ireland continue, and their cumulative economic cost exceeds by a factor of many times the value of all the land in Ireland.

The Puritans are sometimes credited with a literary legacy, but it is not clear that the great literature of the age can be called Puritan. While he had earlier been a member of Parliament's army, John Bunyan apparently did not receive Jesus Christ as his Savior until 1653, after which he became a Baptist and subsequently wrote The Pilgrim's Progress. Even Milton's affiliation is questionable. While a nominal Puritan, Milton advocated free divorce and remarriage when he left his wife. His *De Doctrina Christiana*, published after Milton's death, condoned polygamy as had Martin Luther.[28] This work also rejected orthodox Trinitarianism, a position also taken by Isaac Newton. He advocated a free press when his own works were censored, and reversed this position when he became Cromwell's censor. The Christian theme for *Paradise Lost* was apparently by chance since he considered the pagan Arthurian legends as an alternate topic. Milton's only

---

28. Broadbent 184.

consistency seemed to be in advocating the policies which were in his own immediate self-interest.

The Puritans failed to follow Jesus' instructions that we make ourselves as harmless as doves, but their sins also included idolatry and arrogance. The idolatry was the emphasis on the outward appearance of Christian behavior. The fact that, in their time, the English already had a state religion gives them some excuse which cannot be shared by modern Christians seeking similar political ends. Forcing unbelievers to behave as Christians can only delay their salvation by confusing both unbelievers and evangelists alike. The Bible is quite clear that God wants love, not sacrifice. I do not think that forced behavior can produce love.

Unfortunately, many modern Christians share the Puritans' arrogance. It is the arrogance of assuming one's own interpretation of ambiguous biblical passages is the uniquely correct interpretation. God hates arrogance, so it should never be part of His Holy Sons. The Puritans prayed, read the Bible, and came to the conclusion that infants should be baptized. They were so sure that this conclusion was uniquely correct that they ordered life imprisonment to anyone caught baptizing Christians previously baptized as infants. Most fundamentalists in the United States (including myself) are convinced that the Bible tells us that baptism is a choice which must be made by the person baptized. Lest we be guilty of the same arrogance as the Puritans, we must accept that the contrary beliefs on this and many other matters may be correct. We should treat the holders of those contrary beliefs with Christian love and accept their clear conscience in following those beliefs. Oliver Cromwell persecuted both believers and unbelievers, and his murders are still a barrier to the salvation of many Irish people, but he believed that he was doing the Will of God.

Many of the Puritans were motivated by their love of Christ. With that in mind, we should consider what their legacy would have been if they had sent loving missionaries to Ireland instead of troops, and medical supplies instead of munitions. I believe that the result would have been completely different and that the British Isles would be filled with Bible-believing Puritans today.

E. The American Revolution

The connection of the American Revolution with Christianity is a strained relationship which mostly has been conjured by a few clearly biased authors.

Christianity and Politics

As an example, Sages and Heroes of the American Revolution by E.C. Judson, 1851, states that Thomas Jefferson was a "practical Christian" based on his deeds. Jefferson himself emphatically denied being a Christian throughout his life. In the presidential election of 1800, Jefferson's opponents called him a "howling atheist" and a "confirmed infidel." To call him a Christian is nothing but a distortion of the truth, and it demeans Christ. The other great leader of the Revolution, Benjamin Franklin, was a deist, recognizing only the existence of a non-personal god. The high incidence of deism among the Founding Fathers is indicated by the reference to "Nature and the God of Nature" in the Declaration of Independence. The U.S. Constitution omits any reference to Jesus or the Father, making it a stark contrast with the legal documents of most European nations of the time. Along with Franklin and some of the other leaders of the Revolution, George Washington was a Freemason, and the pagan symbols of that organization remain on the dollar bill and other government emblems.

Some statistics must be taken into account when considering the Christianity of the Revolution. While some Christians have stated that America in the days of the Founding Fathers was almost entirely Christian, this is a hasty conclusion drawn from the fact that only a tiny portion of the population was Jewish. The vast majority of Americans at the time of the Revolution had no religious affiliation. While there were no accurate polls in the eighteenth century, estimates of the portion of Americans who belonged to any church range from 7 percent to a high of 10–15 percent. A French visitor to America at that time observed "religious indifference is imperceptibly disseminated from one end of the continent to another." (*The Godless Constitution*) Venereal disease was so common in the U.S. in the late 1700's and early 1800's that archeologists are able to find the sites of early settlements by the presence of the mercury which was used as a cure for syphilis.[29] It was not a nation of people who had personal relationships with Jesus Christ.

By most accounts, Americans were divided in their support of the Revolution with roughly one third supporting the Revolutionaries, one third opposed (Tories) and about one third indifferent. Fortunately for the Revolutionaries, Britain was also divided on the matter and was at war with France which provided essential aid to the Revolutionaries.[30]

---

29. Orange County Register 9/26/1998.

30. The Whig party of the principal British commanders, cousins Lord General Howe and Lord Admiral Howe, tended to support the Revolution. After their disastrous

The primary religious groups which supported the Revolution were the New Evangelicals, the New Lights, and a few other groups which had Puritan ancestry. The largest group of clergy in the colonies was Anglican, however, and most of that clergy were opposed to the Revolution. The Quakers, Mennonites, and the Brethren were all opposed to the Revolution and some of these Churches were persecuted by the Revolutionaries. Opponents of the Revolution were generally disenfranchised afterwards, and the lands of many (including those who dissented on religious grounds) were confiscated and redistributed among the Revolutionaries.

John Wesley, the founder of the Methodist movement, openly opposed the Revolution writing in "A Calm Address to Our American Colonies" (1775): "But be you not duped any longer; do not ruin yourselves for them that owe you no goodwill, that now employ you only for their own purposes, and in the end will give you no thanks."[31] As a consequence of Wesley's statements, all Methodist ministers (with the sole exception of Francis Asbury) opposed the Revolution.[32]

Wesley's writings on the American Revolution should surprise no one since revolution itself is unChristian. Consider 1 Peter 2:13–15, "Submit yourselves for the Lord's sake to every human institution, whether to a king as the one in authority or to governors as sent by him for the punishment of evildoers and the praise of those who do right for such is the will of God that by doing right you may silence the ignorance of foolish men." Similar messages appear in Romans 13:1–7. Certainly some Christians participated on the side of the Revolutionaries, but it is nothing more than a distortion of the truth to represent the Revolution as a Christian movement.

F. The American Civil War

The Christianity of the American Civil War is similar to that of the American Revolution in that it is little more than a distortion of facts. Both sides of the Civil War claimed that their own side represented Christianity in a struggle against evil. Christian clergy in the South cited Eph 6:5 and Col 3:22 to show that the New Testament approved of slavery, and they said that the abolition of slavery was a conspiracy of unbelievers to make it

---

mismanagement of the British forces, the two Whigs left the final battle and ignominy of surrender to the Tory, General Cornwallis.

31. Ellis Sandoz, *Sermons of the Founding American Evangelists* (Liberty Fund, 1998).
32. Blackwell, *Encyclopedia of the American Revolution*, 1991.

impossible for those commands of the Bible to be followed. Northern clergy cited the jubilees which periodically granted liberty to slaves in Leviticus, the numerous references to liberty in the New Testament, and generally appealed to the inhumanity of enforced servitude. Due to the fact that the Union forces won the war, theirs is the side that is now claimed by most Christians to have represented Christ.

Students of American history know that the Civil War was a conflict of many issues. The North and South had major disputes over both slavery and tariffs. While the issue of slavery receives the most attention today, contemporary commentators such as Charles Dickens believed that the South's reluctance to pay tariffs imposed by the North was the greatest issue. Ultimately, the war was fought over the right of states to secede from the Union. The fact that this issue was resolved on battlefields rather than in courts of law makes it difficult for historians to determine the legitimacy of that right. When the Republic of Texas joined the United States, the right to secede was specifically written into the agreement. Rights to secede were also retained by North Carolina and Virginia when they ratified the Constitution, so it is possible that the legitimacy of secession varied among the states.

The presidential election of 1860 was the impetus for secession. In a four-way split, the Presidential candidate most opposed to slavery, Abraham Lincoln, was elected with 40 percent of the vote while his three opponents split the remaining 60 percent of the votes. For the first two years of the war, the South generally prevailed, and it seemed likely that Britain would recognize the new nation. In order to win support from the abolitionist sympathizers in Britain, Lincoln freed the slaves (in rebelling states only) with the Emancipation Proclamation in 1863. It was a politically costless act for Lincoln since the areas to which the Act applied were not under his control and none of the people affected by the act could vote in the next election.

Abolition of slavery was a favorite cause of many of the Northern clergy, so much so, that some broke the law by aiding the escape of slaves from the South. While only about ten percent of the white families in the South owned any slaves, state and regional loyalties were much stronger than they are today. The illegal transportation of slaves to the North therefore created a great deal of animosity among Southern slave-holders and non-slaveholders alike. The animosity which preceded the Civil War certainly contributed to the haste with which Southern states seceded following the election of the abolitionist Abraham Lincoln.

Analysis

The Civil War was a costly conflict, both in terms of the number of lives lost (about 600,000) and the economic cost. The economic cost of the war, including indirect costs such as the value of time lost by drafted soldiers, is estimated by leading economic historians to have been about $20 billion. These costs of the war do not include the great damage that lingering resentment has caused over the years following the war's end.

The only significant gain from the war was the freeing of the slaves. Of course, this was important since the slavery which persisted in the South, long after it had been abolished throughout the rest of the Western world, was a great injustice.[33]

Let us look at this issue from a Christian perspective. The property rights which existed in the South prior to the 1863 Proclamation allowed people to own slaves. Many Christians wanted those rights rescinded. The attempt to accomplish this by political means resulted in a costly and bloody war. Christians could have accomplished this same ending in a better way.

At the time of the Civil War there were approximately 3 million slaves in the South. The highest price paid for healthy adult male slaves was about $1500. Most slaves were worth far less than this amount. Therefore, the highest realistic estimate that could be put on the economic value of all of the slaves in the U.S is about $4.5 billion. This is less than 25 percent of the economic cost of the Civil War. What would the result have been if Christian assemblies throughout the nation had raised money to buy slaves and set them free? It would certainly have been a much better result than the Civil War. Even if the Christians who were concerned with this issue comprised only 25 percent of the population, it would have been less expensive for those Christians to come up with the money to buy all of the slaves than was the cost of their own participation in the war.

---

33. Preservation of the Union is often presented as a benefit from the Civil War, but this benefit is unclear. There is no reason to believe that people are better off because both the South and the North have the same central government, just as there is no reason to believe that people were better off when both the Ukraine and Russia were part of the Soviet Union as they were prior to the Ukraine's secession. Free trade can take place without political union, and the U.S. has free trade with most of the world today without political control. "Union" is generally the cause of a group of people who want to have political control of another group. It was the slogan of the English who wanted to control Scotland against the will of the Scottish people, and it was the slogan of the North which wanted to control the South against the will of the citizens of the South.

Christianity and Politics

The scenario of Christians raising money to buy slaves one by one and set them free is not unrealistic. It is certainly more Christian than illegally taking those slaves or even trying to free them through political means, and it would probably have been easier. Christian groups today are buying slaves in Northern Africa and setting them free.[34] Purchase and liberation of slaves would not have produced the bitter hatred between the regions and the races which remains today since it would have had no victims. It would have increased respect for Christians and their clergy instead of creating the distrust which came from political activities.

Would it have been fair to a Christian minority to expect them to purchase all of these slaves? Those who ask that question have missed the message of Christianity. It was not fair that Jesus Christ died for us. We are asked to be like Him. Since virtually all political conflicts are disputes over definitions of property rights (this is explained in the chapter "The Economics of Politics"), the opportunity exists for Christians to avert costly battles with acts of charity. We have important opportunities to do this today in domestic areas such as abortion and in international areas such as the Israeli-Palestinian conflict. In all of these areas, the opportunity for charity instead of force is an opportunity to serve Christ and to save souls from the barriers which are inevitably created from violent solutions.

G. World War I

As with many wars, both sides of World War One (WWI) claimed to be the Christian side of the war. German military equipment was generally stamped with the slogan "Gott mit uns" meaning "God is with us." This was taken from the view which was popular in Germany that, as the home of Martin Luther and the Reformation, Germany was a Christian nation which was threatened by Britain and France. Britain, France, Russia, and the US also viewed themselves as Christian nations, and their leaders said that they were fighting a "just war" which would be "the war to end all wars" and would "make the world safe for democracy."

The view that Christians should not participate in war had became more popular in several churches prior to the US participation in WWI. Consequently, politicians who needed men to join the US Army made the argument that "just wars" were an exception to the principle of Christian pacifism, and that the participation by the Allies in WWI was just. In

---

34. Orange County Register 2/8/1998; 4/21/1999.

A Selective History of Christians in Politics

support of that view, Lloyd George, the Prime Minister of Britain, stated on August 4, 1917, "What are we fighting for? To defeat the most dangerous conspiracy ever plotted against the liberty of nations: carefully, skillfully, insidiously, clandestinely planned in every detail, with ruthless, cynical determination." This was part of a speech intended primarily for the benefit of Americans participating in WWI, since the British and other European publics already knew that this was false.

A preponderance of evidence indicates that Britain, France, and Russia had been preparing for WWI for about a decade prior to the war. During the period of 1909–1914, military budgets had increased by 68 percent (for Britain), 147 percent (for France), and a staggering 644 percent for Russia. During this same period, Germany's budget for military expenditures had increased by less than 2 percent and by 1914 it was still less than Britain's budget for military expenditures in 1909. The percentage of GNP spent on military in 1913 was 1.6 percent for Germany. While Britain and France spent 2.3 percent and 3.3 percent respectively in 1911.[35] My principle area of teaching is taxation, and I knowing that new taxes are usually associated with wars. The US enacted its income tax in 1913. In that same year, the US created the Federal Reserve enabling it to issue currency as needed to purchase government debt, thereby enabling the financing of a great war.

Britain's economic motive to participate in WWI was apparent. For most of the nineteenth century, Britain had been the world's leading producer of steel and other heavy manufactured goods. By the late nineteenth century, they were losing that position to Germany. In the 1870s British production of steel was approximately four times as great as that of Germany. Due to Germany's comparative advantage in steel production in the Ruhr Valley, however, by 1910, Britain was importing steel from Germany and by 1914 German steel production exceeded the combined production of Britain, France, and Russia.[36]

If the trend had continued, it would have meant enormous financial losses to some of Britain's wealthiest citizens.

In the US, investment banking syndicates lead by the House of Morgan (through its affiliation with the House of Rothschild) had provided much of the financing for British industry and, as the war progressed, for French

---

35. B.R. Mitchell, *European Historical Statistics* 1750–1970 (New York: Columbia University Press, 1975).

36. Modris Eksteins Lester & Orpen Dennys, Rites of Spring: The Great War and the Birth of the Modern Age, 1989.

and British government bonds, and Morgan was Britain's purchasing agent during the war.[37] The influence which the house of Morgan provided to Britain in the war was made evident as recently as 1987 when Morgan asked Britain to release it from obligations it made for the underwriting of British Petroleum, and stated that its help during the war was a reason for the government of the United Kingdom to now help Morgan.

None of this is meant to represent the side of Germany as innocent in WWI. The eagerness of the Germans to engage in the war is well-known, and Germany's involvement was no less Christian than the participation of the Allies. I am only concentrating on the Allies since their cause is the one, some Christians claim, to have made WWI a just war. As with virtually all wars, both sides participated in treachery as a result of greed. Propaganda was created to induce people to fight. It would have been difficult to manage troops who believed that the purpose of the war was to keep a few dozen British and American capitalists from possibly losing their fortunes. Telling those troops that this was the "war to end all wars" made the task easier. While thousands of Christians in the US adhered to their commitments as peacemakers and many of them were sentenced to death or life imprisonment at hard labor under the Sedition Act (which sentences were commuted to time served in 1921), millions of other Christians were seduced by the concept of a just war and fought, killing others or dying themselves.

In the end, millions of men died, and instead of WWI being the war to end all wars, it precipitated the most violent century in European history. Instead of making the world safe for democracy, the comparatively liberal constitutional monarchies which ruled much of the European continent at the beginning of the twentieth century were replaced with totalitarian dictatorships. The atrocities of World WarII were the aftermath of the severe economic sanctions which were imposed on Germany after WWI. The animosities and disruption which were created by that war continue to threaten Europe, and the influence of investment bankers on the government of the US during WWI continues to produce suspicion of the efficacy of capitalism. The involvement of the House of Rothschild in financing Britain and then, through its US affiliates, helping to persuade the US to join the war was impetus for the animosity which Germans felt for Jews after WWI. Despite the efforts of the few dozen British and American capitalists who believed that they would benefit from the war, the Ruhr Valley's comparative advantage in the production of steel could not be overcome,

---

37. Wikipedia, J.P. Morgan, Jr.

and despite losing two wars, Germany is now Europe's largest producer of automobiles and the European Community's strongest economy.

I am ending my discussion of the history of Christians and politics with WWI. This history was meant to illustrate my point that the involvement of Christians in politics has been a failure, even in the cases which Christians sometimes think are their best political episodes. The ultimate outcomes of more recent events are less certain than the cases from more distant history, so they would provide less help to my case but would have a higher danger of inflaming emotions. The principles, however, remain the same. Greed and racism drive politics. The politicians need the support of Christians to vote, man their armies, and pay taxes to the state. To garner that support, they invent convincing stories that the current issues are different and that Christian involvement will serve Christ. Unfortunately, many Christians continue to be duped by those stories.

3

The Economics of Politics

"But you have now rejected your God, who saves you out of all your disasters and calamities. And you have said, 'No, appoint a king over us.' So now present yourselves before the LORD by your tribes and clans." (1 Sam 10:19)

POLITICS IS THE STRUGGLE for control of government. That struggle generally has the intention of changing laws for the benefit of the victors in the political struggle. The tools of politics include military force, rebellion, voting, and persuasion. The principal political struggle in the Bible is a struggle in which man resists God's will. It is a story of rebellion. This began in Eden, where man disobeyed God, temporarily giving his soul to an evil influence. He was duped by Satan into participating in a rebellion which was doomed to failure. Man was not an active contender so much as a temporary victim in this struggle. This continuing struggle is much of the story in the Old Testament.

In the modern world, the struggle of politics remains one of men contending with God's Law. As with all personal conflicts, it is only an illusion that men are contending with each other. They are actually contending with God's Law, and not loving their neighbors as themselves is part of that. Hence, modern political struggles are no different from the conflict in the Garden of Eden. Men contend with each other in the political arena because each is seeking his own will and is ignoring the Will of God.

Politics has become so much a part of modern society that social scientists attempt to justify it with theories showing that politics is a necessary tool for the solution of social problems, and many people today believe those theories. This chapter will instead show that:

The Economics of Politics

1. Participation in politics is not in keeping with God's plan for the rule of man.
2. Changing laws amounts to changing property rights. This activity is a form of theft which possibly makes some people richer and certainly makes others poorer.
3. In a relatively free society (such as the United States) politics are not necessary for solving social problems since judicial systems and voluntary contracts are able to solve those problems in a way that is economically superior to political solutions.
4. Because of the three points above, Christians should only participate in politics when the issue involves a God-given Christian right (such as worship, prayer, or witnessing). AND that right cannot be obtained through the courts or through voluntary transactions with other parties. This means that Christians should not participate in politics in relatively free societies like the United States.

In the Garden of Eden, man sought to eat fruit from the Tree of Knowledge of Good and Evil when the right to eat that fruit did not belong to man. This attempt at taking God's rights and transferring those rights to themselves was the rebellion of man.

While God gave the Israelites rules for appointing kings, the Bible makes it clear that this was not God's first choice. God's first intention was that, through his Son Jesus, he would be the King of Israel. I Samuel 8: 6 states "But when they said, "Give us a king to lead us," this displeased Samuel; so he prayed to the Lord. And the Lord told him: "Listen to all that the people are saying to you; it is not you they have rejected, but they have rejected me as their king." Then, in verse I Sam 8:19–22, "But the people refused to listen to Samuel. "No!" they said. "We want a king over us. Then we will be like all the other nations, with a king to lead us and to go out before us and fight our battles." When Samuel heard all that the people said, he repeated it before the Lord. 22 The Lord answered, "Listen to them and give them a king."

Telling Samuel to give Israel a King was similar to the Lord telling Moses to give the Israelites rules for divorce or His instructing Solomon how to build the temple.

Jesus tells us that his Father never intended that people should get divorced. Nonetheless, he gave the Israelites rules for divorce since he knew the hardness of their hearts. (Mt 19:8). Anyone who reads Leviticus carefully should see that God does not ever tell people to divorce their wives. He only gives rules that protect the wives that are divorced, knowing that this crime against marriage will take place.

This is similar to the instructions for building Solomon's temple. God says that he cannot live in a temple built by human hands. His clear intention is to live in the temple built by Jesus—the bodies of Christian believers. He told Samuel in 2 Sam 7:5–16 "Go and tell my servant David, This is what the Lord says: 'Are you the one to build me a house to dwell in? I have not dwelt in a house from the day I brought the Israelites up out of Egypt to this day. I have been moving from place to place with a tent as my dwelling. Wherever I have moved with all the Israelites, did I ever say to any of their rulers whom I commanded to shepherd my people Israel, "Why have you not built me a house of cedar?" Now then, tell my servant David, "This is what the Lord Almighty says: I took you from the pasture, from tending the flock, and appointed you ruler over my people Israel. I have been with you wherever you have gone, and I have cut off all your enemies from before you. Now I will make your name great, like the names of the greatest men on earth. And I will provide a place for my people Israel and will plant them so that they can have a home of their own and no longer be disturbed. Wicked people will not oppress them anymore, as they did at the beginning and have done ever since the time I appointed leaders over my people Israel. I will also give you rest from all your enemies."

"The LORD DECLARES TO YOU THAT THE LORD HIMSELF WILL ESTABLISH A HOUSE FOR YOU: When your days are over and you rest with your ancestors, I will raise up your offspring to succeed you, your own flesh and blood, and I will establish his kingdom. He is the one who will build a house for my Name, and I will establish the throne of his kingdom forever. I will be his father, and he will be my son. When he does wrong, I will punish him with a rod wielded by men, with floggings inflicted by human hands. But my love will never be taken away from him, as I took it away from Saul, whom I removed from before you. Your house and your kingdom will endure forever before me; your throne will be established forever.'"

It should be clear to any Christian reading these passages that the Lord did not want David or any other mortal to build a house for him. That was reserved for Jesus of whom the Lord says "your house and your kingdom will endure forever before me." Nonetheless, The Lord gave instructions to David and Solomon for the manmade temple which he knew that they would build.

The Economics of Politics

The anointing of Israel's kings is similar. We know that all glory and power is reserved for Jesus Christ. I Samuel 10:17 tells us that asking for a king was an evil thing. "... you will realize what an evil thing you did in the eyes of the LORD when you asked for a king."

And 1 Sam 12:19 says: "The people all said to Samuel, 'Pray to the LORD your God for your servants so that we will not die, for we have added to all our other sins the evil of asking for a king.'"

While this was an evil thing, robbing God of the glory which belonged to Him, God permitted the Israelites to make this mistake and then gave them instructions for the anointing of kings.

Prior to the anointing of King Saul, the administration of Israel's government was in the hands of judges, who were directly appointed by God. The laws of God provided unchanging definitions of property rights, and the judges administered God's laws. While they administered laws, they did not rule by making new laws. As Gideon said (Judges 8:23) "I will not rule over you, nor will my son rule over you. The Lord will rule over you." The introduction of kings to Israel is described in chapter 8 of I Samuel. God had not appointed a king over Israel, but the people of Israel demanded one. By this process, God said that the Israelites had forsaken him and were serving other gods (I Samuel 7:7–8). The kings in the Bible wrote new laws (as referenced in Ezra 7:26), and this is a distinction between the kings and the judges. By writing laws, the king is taking God's place. It should be evident to Christians that God's plan from the beginning was that Jesus Christ would be the King of all the earth. When we seek someone else as our king, we attempt to take what belongs to God.

God told Samuel to warn the people of the consequences of a king, but Israel still asked for a king, and it received one, along with the consequence of political struggle. Christians who use politics to change the world are forsaking the Lord in a similar manner. They are giving up on Christ as king and seeking to have a man as their king. They are refusing to use the Christian tools of evangelism, prayer, charity and being good examples, and relying instead on the way of the world. This is the reasoning behind my first point for this chapter: that participation in politics is not part of God's first plan for His people.

Let me now present the second part of this chapter showing that changing laws amounts to a legalized form of theft. Laws define our property rights. While most people think of property as a physical object, property is really a bundle of rights. When someone acquires a physical object, the buyer receives the right to do certain things with that object, but does not receive the right to do other things. For example, if you buy a radio, you have the right to listen to the radio but, in most communities, you do not have the right to play it so loudly that it produces more than 70 decibels of sound at the edge of your neighbor's property. Your neighbor owns the right to not have more than 70 decibels of sound at the edge of his property, and if you produce more sound than that, you are violating your neighbor's property rights. As another example, the ownership of land along a river may or may not include various rights to use the river. It might include some rights (such as the right to swim or fish) but not other rights (such as the right to alter the flow of water or pollute the river). Similarly, a law may prohibit the owner of land from cutting the trees on that land. The law is not taking the trees from the landowner. It is simply saying that some rights regarding the trees belong to other people.

For the most part, changes in laws are change in definitions of property rights. For example, laws that are passed to limit what someone can build on land that he owns amount to a transfer of part of the bundle of rights which the owner of that land acquired at the time of purchase. Laws which prohibit possession of a firearm in certain public places take away part of the bundle of rights which is otherwise associated with owning that firearm. The person who previously held those rights loses them with the change in law while some other person or persons gain the rights. From this perspective, changes in law are a form of legal theft. One person is taking what previously belonged to another person. This is why politics is required for changing laws, and it is why politics is often brutal. It always has a potential loser who will generally use all the means at his disposal to keep from losing. It has a contra-party to the loser, but that contra-party may not be a winner since the contra-party will spend his own resources in his attempt to win. Due to miscalculations, the party which is contra to the loser may spend more resources in trying to win than is the value of the prize.

There is a net loss to society from political activity, just as there is a net loss to society from illegal theft. Both the thief and the defender willingly expend their own resources up to the value of the object which is stolen, yet nothing new is produced. Consequently, the anticipated social cost of the illegal theft is up to two times the value of the object which might be stolen. As political participants avail themselves of every means possible to win, the social cost of politics may reach this same level. This is the reasoning for my second point that changing laws through politics is a form of theft.

My third point is that in a relatively free society (such as the United States) politics are not necessary for solving social problems since judicial systems and voluntary contracts are able to solve those problems in a way that is economically superior to political solutions. Usually, when social scientists are told that problems normally resolved by politics can be resolved with voluntary contracts and judicial solutions, they state that this is not so when externalities exist.

Externalities are situations in which private costs and/or benefits of an activity are different than the social costs and/or benefits of the activity. The mainstream theory in social sciences is that when externalities are present, political solutions are necessary to produce socially desirable allocations of resources. This is at odds with the unchanging laws of God, and it is therefore wrong. While Christians should be content with a system of unchanging laws, they may be comforted to learn that good economics supports this system. The economist and legal theorist Ronald Coase wrote about the use of voluntary contracts to resolve problems which are normally considered political, and for this work he received a well-deserved Nobel Prize in Economics.[1] Coase's seminal article in this area was entitled "The Problem of Social Cost." In essence, this work deals with the topic of whether some problems which most people believe to require political solutions could be optimally handled by a court system with properly defined and easily transferable property rights.

The problem of social cost deals with situations in which the social costs (or benefits) of someone's actions are greater (or less) than the private costs (or benefits) of the actor. The classic case of social cost is pollution. The owner of a factory may, for example, need to choose between two methods of production. One method is less expensive, but it requires polluting a nearby river. While the harm to society from the pollution exceeds the benefits of this first production method, the factory owner only bears a small part of the costs of pollution since those are a "social cost." The second method leaves no pollution but is more expensive in terms of the costs paid by the factory owner.

In the traditional analysis of this problem the profit-maximizing factory owner chooses the less expensive method, thereby creating social cost. This choice is inefficient from the view of society as a whole (since the cost of the pollution exceeds the savings to the factory owner) but since, in this

---

1. Ronald Coase, "The Problem of Social Cost" *Journal of Law and Economics,* Oct 1960.

traditional analysis, the factory owner responds only to his personal incentives, he chooses this method anyway. Consequently, the traditional analysis of this problem requires government intervention to stop the pollution.

In his paper, Coase shows that if people can freely transact with each other, then the result will be an optimal allocation of resources regardless of which party initially owns any property rights. For example, in the case of the river which the factory owner wants to pollute, some party owns the rights to the use of the river for this purpose. If those rights are owned by the factory owner giving him the right to pollute, then a single landowner who is downstream from the factory may attempt to buy those rights from the factory owner. He will buy the rights if receiving unpolluted water has more value to him than what the factory owner saves by the production process which pollutes. The exact price may be something which is negotiated, but if the value of those rights to the downstream owner exceeds the value to the factory owner, we may be sure that some transaction will eventually take place

What if the savings to the factory owner exceeds the value to the downstream property owner from receiving unpolluted water? In that case, it is socially optimal that the factory owner pollute. In some cases, like this one, pollution is part of an optimal solution, and a strict prohibition of all pollution would not be in the best interest of society. It is inevitable that some types of pollution will take place. What is important is that pollution only takes place when the benefits exceed the costs.

The same results would take place if the rights to whether or not the water is clean are initially owned by the downstream property owner. If the savings to the factory owner from polluting are less than the cost of the pollution to the downstream property owner, then the factory owner will not be willing to offer enough money or other consideration to buy those rights. Alternatively, if the factory owner's savings from polluting exceed the cost of the pollution to the downstream property owner, then he will be willing to offer enough to buy the rights to pollute the water. Coase's point is that with clearly defined and freely transferrable property rights, the costs and savings from pollution are what determine whether or not the pollution will take place. If all of the property rights are transferable, then any consistent set of property right definitions by courts will allow private parties to make transactions which result in the most desired uses of the property (at least in the case of two party conflicts.) The initial ownership of property rights is irrelevant. A political resolution is unnecessary and, in fact, is likely to be destructive.

Increasing the number of landowners along the river makes the problem more complicated due to what is called a "free-rider" problem. This problem does not need to destroy the practical implications of Coase's theorem as long as judicial systems allow sufficiently complex definitions of property rights, and even with simple judicial rules, it should not destroy the implications for Christians.

The free-rider problem is that in a situation in which many different people would benefit from the same action and cannot be compelled to pay for that action, then each person has an incentive to not contribute. The non-contributors would benefit without paying and would therefore be "free riders." In the example of a factory owner who pollutes a river, there could be several downstream property owners, each of whom would benefit from the river not being polluted. Even if the collective benefit to the downstream property owners exceeds the costs to the factory owner from not polluting, each of those downstream property owners might wait for the other property owners to pay the factory owner and avoid payment himself. Consequently, the free-rider problem presents an externality which is not resolved as simply as the situation in which there are only two parties.

One solution to the free-rider problem is to allow courts to define property rights in a way which aggregates costs and benefits. For example, property rights could be defined so that each free rider had an obligation to pay for benefits. Complex (but consistent) definitions of property rights lead to other solutions as well, but it is beyond the scope of this book to discuss those. These are all examples of what is popularly called "judicial activism." While judicial activism is a substitute for political activity, if it is applied with consistent and predictable rules, then it is not re-defining property rights. It is only applying more complex rules to determine the bundle of rights which is owned by each participant. Often those more complex rules are necessary to resolve issues of property which were previously unknown. Judicial activism is necessary to allow rules for property rights when new technology creates situations not previously litigated. For example, in A.M. Records vs. Napster, Inc. 239 F.3d 1004 (2001) the Ninth Circuit Court of Appeals made a ruling which held Napster liable for copyright infringements by its users. In essence, the court aggregated the liabilities of many individual participants. The Ninth Circuit Court of Appeals similarly acted to aggregate and divide costs of copyright infringement in Universal City

Studios v. Sony F.2d 963 (9th Cir. 1981). While that case was later reversed by the US Supreme Court, (464 U.S. 417, 1984) the reversal was for reasons not related to the aggregation.

In a more general application against free riders, courts have held all members of a class which benefits from a class action lawsuit may be liable for a share of legal costs. Following these principles, all of the benefits from other free rider problems could be held liable for their share of costs.

While judicial activism has the potential to resolve problems of free riders, Christians should not need to rely on this. When there is a social issue of importance to Christians, Christians can join together to buy the property rights that they need. Christians can also participate in voluntary solutions to issues which are not Christian in nature but which are simply good causes. While it is possible that Christians are free-riders on some secular issues, no Christian is a true free-rider on a Christian issue. We know that while forgiven, we will someday stand before Jesus Christ who will know and perfectly understand all of our actions and intentions. The fact that it is not our business to be concerned with what others receive is a recurrent theme of the New Testament. This allows for no free riders, and every Christian should be willing to do the work which helps Christianity

What about the case in which free-riders are not Christians? In that case, Christians have the opportunity to make themselves good witnesses by ignoring the economic problem that unbelievers are free-riders. In many situations the potential benefits from the charitable act of paying for the costs of externalities while ignoring free-rider problems are enormous. In the chapter on history, I described how a relatively small number of Christians could have bought all of the slaves in the South and freed them for a cost which was less than those Christians paid for the Civil War. Wars are often like that. Relatively small costs which no one wants to pay individually can lead to a war which costs hundreds of times as much as the costs in dispute. Every Christian is a free-rider on the costs paid by Jesus Christ. It is his will that ALL should be saved, so we should not bear ill will towards any person who benefits from our own petty endeavors without bearing a share of the costs. As stated in 1Peter 2:12 "Keep your behavior excellent among the Gentiles, so that in the thing in which they slander you as evildoers, they may, on account of your good deeds as they observe them, glorify God in the day of visitation."

4

The Nature of Politics

". . . you are all brothers." (Mt 23:8)

THE DISCUSSION OF EXTERNALITIES in the previous chapter shows that political solutions are unnecessary re-definitions of property rights. Politics is therefore a less than zero-sum game. The solutions which may be obtained through judicial processes generally will be more advantageous to mankind. Politics does not give the best solutions, and the laws of man are not the results of enlightened attempts to serve society.

Political scientists, economists, and academicians who study other areas as well generally use paradigms to aid in their analyses. A paradigm is a model which can be used to better understand otherwise unexplained phenomena. Newton's Laws of Motion, for example, comprise a paradigm which was, and is still, helpful in understanding movement in the physical universe. The fact that Einstein's view of the universe shows that Newton's model is incorrect, does not stop Newton's model from being useful. Understanding the various paradigms which are used to explain political behavior can help to understand why educated people have differing opinions.

Throughout history, philosophers have developed many different paradigms on politics and government. According to the modern social scientist's paradigm, politics is the means by which the best obtainable solutions to social problems are determined. Under this paradigm political participants are enlightened people who intend to serve the best interest of society. It states that, in a pluralistic democracy, no one person is consistently a loser through the political processes, and each person has a net gain from politics. The modern social scientist's paradigm further states that the bargains which are eventually struck through political compromises represent the best solutions which are achievable.

The modern social scientist's paradigm of government cannot be found anywhere in the Bible simply because it is unbiblical. It is also not valid. The social scientists' model of government begins with the assumption that politicians seek to serve the best interests of other people. This is a view which is unrealistic and also unbiblical since the Bible teaches us that men are selfish. Like most people, politicians serve their own selfish material ends. The fact that those who seek to do no harm have nothing to fear from these political authorities (Romans 13:4) is simply an outcome of the selfish behavior of government authorities. They need people to serve them and it would only hinder their own interests to oppress those who obey the law.

In general, the motivation of those involved in the political process is not the good of society. No one can claim that the Normans invaded Britain to provide better government to the Anglo-Saxons. Even William the Conqueror admitted (on his deathbed) that he had no right to invade England and did it only for selfish ambition. While this is immediately obvious to any good historian, the fact that the winners of any political contest seek only to further their own ends becomes equally obvious to the close observer who spends time to reflect on facts. The failure of the social scientists' paradigm to provide a genuine motivation for politics is important for understanding Christian participation since it means that politics are not part of a well-designed process which serves the best interests of mankind. While Christians are told to obey rulers because "there is no authority except from God" (Romans 13:1–7), this does not imply that the political process is godly, only that God directs its outcome.

In this chapter I will:

1. present a paradigm for understanding politics based on biological survival
2. explain how some people use this paradigm to justify selfish political acts which result in their competitors not surviving
3. explain that the use of the biological paradigm to justify selfishness at the expense of others is logically flawed and that brotherly love is more rational than selfishness even within the biological paradigm
4. explain why showing brotherly love requires overcoming our biological instincts

Among modern worldly thinkers, the leading paradigm on government and politics is a paradigm based on evolution and the applications of biology to social behavior or, as it is sometimes called, sociobiology. While the social scientists' paradigms are unable to explain government and politics, the paradigm of sociobiology offers a solution. This is a paradigm originating in the works of Spencer and Darwin. Not all believers in evolution believe in this paradigm, and it is never stated by Darwin. Nonetheless, it is probably the most influential paradigm for worldly people. Like the social scientists' paradigm it is useful for Christians to understand in determining our own participation. It is particularly useful to understand because this paradigm probably explains more of the worldly motivation for politics than any other model.

The basis for the sociobiologists' paradigm lies in the animal world. Within the animal world individual members of any species compete for survival with the other members of the species. The strongest members win the competition. Social species (such as wolves) will sometimes isolate weaker members of their pack, preventing them from breeding or even sharing food. This behavior is good for the long-run survival of the species, since it results in stronger and healthier members in each generation. The evolutionists have integrated this behavior into their theories of gene survival, and this integrated theory is used by a subset of evolutionists called sociobiologists.

The sociobiologists' paradigm takes the pattern for social behavior in animals and expands it into a theory which explains human behavior and competition as both outcomes and continuations of the evolutionary process. In essence, the theory is as follows:

1. All life forms are the outcome of competition for survival.

2. This competition for survival is ultimately won by the life forms which exhibit selfish behavior.

3. War and politics are the methods by which selfish humans compete with each other for survival

This philosophy of selfishness is probably a greater threat to the world than the social scientists' paradigm of government for the simple reason that it is apparent to any careful observer that some parts of the evolutionists' paradigm are true. Many worldly politicians use the social scientists' paradigm as a way to dupe their subjects, but they actually believe in the sociobiologists' paradigm. Since the paradigm assumes that all living things behave in a selfish manner, it has many behavioral implications that are true. The persistence of this selfish behavior is seen by the sociobiologists as evidence of the validity of their theory, so it is my second point of this chapter, that the paradigm of sociobiology is used by some people to justify their own selfish acts.

While it surprises the social scientist, it should be no surprise to the Christian that the motivation of politics is one of selfishness. James 4:2 tells us that we fight and quarrel because we are envious and cannot obtain, and this fighting and quarreling is what politics is all about. Since the Bible tells us that we are selfish, Christians know that parts of the paradigm derived from biology and the Theory of Evolution are true. We have selfish instincts. That is part of man's nature. In fact, as far as human behavior goes, I do not know of any observed implications for behavior from the sociobiologists' paradigm which cannot simply be explained by the statements that man is selfish, but he loves his family members, both of which are biblical.

While parts of the sociobiologists' paradigm are true, other parts are not. Both the Bible and the sociobiologists can explain man's selfish behavior, but only the New Testament can explain the selfless behavior of Christians who are filled with the Holy Spirit. This selfless behavior is not part of the old man, who dies when a person receives Jesus Christ as his Savior, and it is our proof of the failure of the sociobiologists' paradigm. Our selfish nature is of this world, but that does not make it good or beneficial to mankind. In fact, this selfish behavior would destroy mankind if Christ did not come in time to save us. Because worldly politicians rely on the paradigm of selfish behavior, they are overcome by the selfless behavior of Christian martyrs. 1John 5:4 "For whatever is born of God overcomes the world; and this is the victory that has overcome the world, our faith." Worldly politicians are totally unprepared for this behavior and have no way of controlling it.

In order to better understand the sociobiologists' theory and its failings, we should look into its philosophical history. Many Christians think only of the theories of Charles Darwin when they hear the term "evolution," but evolution is a philosophical tool that helps to better understand many subjects that have no direct relationship with biology. The nineteenth-century philosopher, Herbert Spencer, wrote and lectured on the topic of evolution's applications to general problems of the universe and particularly to social institutions. Today, Spencer is often called the inventor of

Social Darwinism with the inference that Spencer had taken a model which was developed by Darwin and attempted to apply it to human relationships. Spencer's writings on applications of evolution, however, pre-date Darwin and cover a wide variety of topics in addition to social behavior. Spencer wrote *The Theory of Population* in 1852 and stated in this work that the "struggle for existence" resulted in the "survival of the fittest," apparently making the first printed use of those phrases. Darwin began writing his work *On the Origin of Species* in 1856, and the abstract was first published in November of 1859. Darwin's first public presentation of his theory of evolution was in a joint paper with Alfred Russell Wallace in 1858, so it is virtually impossible that Darwin influenced Spencer's early work. Both authors were probably influenced by Jean Baptiste Lamarck, who described a theory of biological evolution in his *Zoological Philosophy* which was published in 1809. The relative dates of their writing and Spencer's coverage of a broad range of applications of evolution indicate, however, that it would be more appropriate to call Darwin a Biological Spencerist than it is to call Spencer a Social Darwinist.[1]

The point of this is that the application of theories of evolution to a wide variety of subjects does not borrow from Darwin. Darwin's contribution was only a very specific theory of biological evolution based on randomly occurring mutations. Modern writers have used theories of evolution to explain sociobiology, and the applications of this to human behavior have only brought the philosophy of evolution back to Spencer's theories.

Evolution, as described by Spencer, is a process through which simpler forms are transformed into more complex forms. This is a theory with general applications, and it is not limited to forms of life. This general theory of evolution can be applied to astronomy, business, or any other area of study in which the forms which exist at some early point in time are affected by a continuing process so that they evolve into more complex forms at a later point in time.

---

1. Part of the nearly universal academic acceptance of Darwin's theory must be attributed to the fact that it relies on randomness. Randomness is really a statement which means that we are unable to find a predictable mechanism for the formation of mutations which result in new species. This makes Darwin's theory an excellent example of a null hypothesis, and the acceptance of Darwin's theory by scientists is primarily a statement that scientists are unable to find a predictable mechanism which creates new species. This does not mean that no such mechanism exists, only that scientists are unable to find it.

Survival is an essential part of the system. According to Spencer, various forces of nature allow appropriately modified forms to survive, while the simpler forms do not survive. What we see at any point of time is the result of what previously existed, the transforming process, and the process that allows some forms to survive while other forms do not. When evolution is stated in this general form, it is easy to find applications to business, government or any other dynamic social institution. Since the Bible tells us that we are not in chaos, evolution (in a general sense) is consistent with Christian beliefs. One Christian application of evolution is that influence from the Holy Spirit is a process affecting Christians. The new Christian is a simple form. Influence from the Holy Spirit, either directly or through other Christians and the Word of God, creates the more complex form of a mature Christian. The choices of Christians to follow the direction of the Holy Spirit and Scriptures eventually bring death to the old man and create the man who is "born again." At any point of time, what we observe is a function of the person as he was on the date he was saved, the changing force of the Holy Spirit, and the choice of the Christian to let the old self die. The process continues and expands as Christians follow Christ's commandments to witness to others, thereby letting the Holy Spirit enter more willing souls.

Let us return to the sociobiologists' theory of social behavior. As Spencer observed, the world is "a struggle for existence" which results only in the "survival of the fittest." In the undeveloped world of primitive man, the efforts of man could not increase the supply of food and the other necessities of life. In this pre-agrarian world, men hunted and gathered the food which was produced by nature. Once they were hunting and gathering to the best of their abilities, there was nothing else that could increase the food supply. If there were a war or epidemic which destroyed part of the population, the natural birthrate would fully restore the population over a period of time which was short relative to the milestones of natural history. Similarly, if the supply of food fell during those wars or epidemics, it was quickly restored to its old level by natural processes.

The relatively fixed supply of food along with a natural birthrate of more than two per mother meant that the supply of food was the principal binding constraint on the long-run growth in population and, in the primitive world of hunters and gatherers the supply of food was more or less constant over the long run. Due to the lack of extra food, the population could not grow. If any behavior could increase the likelihood of someone and his

The Nature of Politics

progeny obtaining food (and therefore being among the survivors), then we would expect to see that behavior appear among survivors. That is the core of the sociobiologists' theory of politics, my first point of this chapter.

If the supply of food is fixed, then the population which that food supply supports must be at least approximately fixed. Any new behavior could only increase the likelihood of survival for the new behavior's holders by decreasing the likelihood of survival for those who do not hold the new behavior. Under Darwinian evolution in which new variations in behavior are not likely to be shared with the other members of a species, a successful new variation in behavior may be one which is entirely at the expense of the other specie members which do not have the mutation. (This success of mutants at the expense of the rest of the population would not be necessary in Lamarkian evolution, but I am ignoring Lamark's model since the Darwinian model is so widely accepted.) For example, there may be a mutation which causes its holders to destroy the specie members which lack the mutation. Such a mutation may form since all of the formations under Darwinian evolution are random. Once that mutation formed, it would be likely to survive since it would destroy all of the specie members which lacked the mutation.

Under some assumptions, the species is better off (as measured by more offspring being able to survive) due to the aggressive behavior of new mutations against the other members of the species.

Assume:
1. a pre-agrarian society in which people support themselves by hunting for wild game
2. that the supply of wild game at the beginning of each year is constant
3. that good hunters can support more people with the same supply of wild game than inferior hunters can support with the same supply of wild game
4. that the traits which make someone a good hunter are the same traits which make the person good at war and political oppression
5. that those traits are inheritable by offspring

Under these five assumptions, more people will be supported in a society in which the good hunters oppress the weaker members of the species, resulting in fewer of those weak people's offspring surviving. If "more people" is the goal of society and is therefore the measure of what is good, then it is better for society that the strong oppress the weak. It is internal politics when the stronger members of the group choose to help themselves at the expense of the weaker members of the same group. It is external politics when the group chooses to help themselves at the expense of another group.

Since social value in this sort of society is based on physical strength, the participants are likely to consist solely of adult males. If the adult males are approximately equal in their power, then this may lead to democracy, so it is not surprising that societies which lacked sophisticated weaponry were essentially democratic.

This model of political behavior is consistent with much of the political behavior which is observable in mankind. The evolutionists' theory implies that a healthy, normal majority will oppress a weaker and stranger minority. Evolutionists' politics in a primitive society may mean forming a coalition of those who make the best teams at hunting and defending, and excluding the less able from the "meat pot" after the hunt . This is similar to the pattern of behavior which is observed in packs of wolves. Similarly, in modern societies, men want to establish affinities with the rich and the powerful while disassociating themselves from the poor and the weak so that they wind up as a part of the political coalition which selects who may and may not survive. If the poor and weak are easily identified by a characteristic such as skin color, and, especially if that characteristic is passed on to their descendants, then the affiliations of the rich and powerful become racism.

Nietzsche provides a philosophical extension of the sociobiologists' behavioral model. Nietzsche says that it makes no sense to desire that which cannot survive, and if the strong survive while the weak do not, then strength is desirable while weakness is not. If oppressing the weak improves the chances of the strong, then oppression is good. Nietzsche praises the strong and urges them to oppress the weak. It is a natural conclusion of worldly evolution. In fact, this is the greatest danger of the theory of evolutionary origins of man because through Nietzsche's logic the theory of evolution implies that the only purpose of life is survival and that is obtained by oppressing other people. It is a direct attack on the divine purpose of life and on Christian behavior. It should not be surprising that Nietzsche and his philosophies were explicitly anti-Christian and some of Nietzsche's writings are little more than attacks on Christianity. Nietzsche's philosophy

The Nature of Politics

does a better job of describing worldly politics than do the theories of social science that look for the common good.

Let us take a deeper look at the sociobiolgists' model of politics. The sociobiologists' model assumed that the food supply was fixed. If we are talking about animals, or even about humans in a pre-agrarian society, this is a reasonable assumption, and it is why political competition among wolves and other social animals is good for the species. The survivors of the political competition are likely to produce offspring which will make better use of the fixed supply of food available to the wolves. This is not a reasonable assumption, however, for humans in the modern world. It would not have been reasonable even in the times of the biblical patriarchs. For thousands of years, the supply of food and the other essentials of life have been highly variable. Those essentials of life have increased at a fairly rapid rate due to capital investments which converted wilderness into farms and due to improvements of technology. The population of the world has grown at an increasingly rapid rate so that it now doubles in a period of less than forty years.

For the past thousand years, the rate of growth in the population has been influenced by the amount of resources devoted to improving the production of food. Political conflicts have reduced the ability of the population to grow in two ways. First, the political conflicts consumed resources that could have been used to increase the production of food. Plowshares were made into swords. Second, the political conflicts destroyed developments which had already been made. Cities were burnt and irrigation systems destroyed. As a consequence of these hindrances to economic growth, the growth in the world's food supply and population are irreversibly set back. In other words, centuries after the conclusion of a war, the total production of food is still lower than it would have been without the war.

The permanent reduction in the population due to war and other political conflicts is at odds with the justification of the sociobiology-view of politics. This is because the sociobiologists' theory is based on a primitive society in which the actions of man had no long-run effects on the food supply. The pre-agrarian society produced approximately the same amount of food whether a war took place or not, so the population would quickly return to the level which preceded any war. In the modern world, however, the available food supply is the result of man's efforts, and particularly man's investment in agriculture and food processing. If those investments are destroyed, the food supply falls as a consequence. While people may continue to make investments in agriculture and food processing so that the food supply is eventually restored to pre-war levels, those same new investments could have been made without a war in which case the food supply would have been brought to even higher levels. Therefore, while we may restore the food supply to its pre-war level, it is unlikely that that we will ever bring it up to the same level that it would have been at the current point of time if no war had ever taken place. As a consequence, relative to the population levels which would have prevailed without a war, war causes a permanent reduction in the population of the modern world.

It would be difficult to estimate the extent to which the growth in the resources which support human survival has been slowed by overtly selfish behavior. It is certainly substantial. By the standards of world history, the United States in the late-twentieth century has been a peaceful nation with a rapidly improving standard of living. Even so, the resources devoted to the military each year (about 2.8 percent of GNP in the de-militarized late 1990s) are more than net capital investment. If we also include the costs of maintaining police and law enforcement which are required due to the overtly selfish behavior of some of the population, the cost of selfishness increases. If we include the private costs of avoiding fraud and other thefts, (virtually all accounting costs, financial transactions costs, etc.) then we have costs which total between 25 percent and 50 percent of the U.S. Gross Domestic Product, or ten to twenty times the amount of net capital investment. Of course, economists generally assume that there are decreasing marginal returns to investment. Even then, an extremely conservative rough estimate would be that the growth rate in production of resources necessary for human survival in the United States would double if the resources wasted by selfish efforts were invested. For most of the world and for most of history, the costs of selfish behavior have been even greater than in the United States in the late twentieth century, so a doubling of the growth rate is even more conservative for the rest of the world as an estimate of the long run benefits which would have been obtained by Christian instead of selfish behavior. If the growth rate in the world's economy had doubled even a century ago, it would be possible for everyone in the world to be very wealthy by today's standards.

Having established that selfish behavior is socially costly, there remains the question of whether the selfish behavior is individually costly to the perpetrators. After all, the theory of evolution implies that an action which has social cost but individual gains may still take place, at least over the short run. While this is irrelevant for the Christian's own behavior, the prospect of personal gain at great social cost may still appeal to the non-believer.

Let us first answer this question from the sociobiologists' own perspective. Sociobiology is based on evolution and on Darwinian evolution in particular. Its selfish adherent wants his own genes to survive, rather than the genes of other people. The genetic structure of all men is, however, very similar. While no two people (other than identical twins) are likely to have exactly the same genetic structure, most of the genes of each person are shared by every other person. Furthermore, there are probably no people who possess any genes which are not shared by millions of other people. Under any popular theory of biological evolution it would take many generations for one set of genes to replace another set in the genetic code of man. Many generations of the social costs created by overtly selfish behavior would reduce the world's economic output to a small fraction of what it could otherwise attain. Since the world's population is dependent on the amount of the resources of the world which are able to support the population, after a long period of this selfish behavior the population would be much smaller than the population would be without that behavior. Hence, in an effort to realize an increased percentage incidence of some gene which the selfish person carries, this person (and his descendants) must for many generations act in a way that reduces the world population. That means that his actions reduce the survival rates for many people who carry the same genes which he carries. Since the percentage of permanent reduction in the world population is likely to be greater than the percentage increase in the incidence of any particular genes carried by the destructively selfish person, this person will have fewer descendants and each of his own genes will be less prevalent than if he had behaved in a socially productive manner. In other words, genes that encouraged destructive selfish behavior would eventually destroy their own chances for survival.

This is my third point, the logical flaw in the sociobiologists' justification of aggressive behavior. The facts that aggression through either war or politics irrevocably destroys the resources necessary for survival, and the fact that people have so many genetic similarities that destruction of any group of people is certain to diminish the survival chances of any of the genes of the aggressor, mean that the selfish aggressor hurts himself.

The Christian perspective gives the same conclusion in a simpler manner. All men are brothers. It would be foolish to obstruct your brother's success because it makes your own relative success greater. The sun and rain benefit everyone (Mt 5:45) so we should want to help our brothers. The general prosperity which results helps us more than we could ever benefit by trying to destroy our brothers. We know that the meek will survive, because Jesus said so in the Sermon on the Mount (Mt 5:5), "The meek will inherit the earth."[2] "Those who live by the sword will die by the sword." Anyone who believes differently has only deluded himself. As stated in 1 Cor 1:19, "I will destroy the wisdom of the wise, and the cleverness of the clever I will set aside."

If political aggression is harmful to the aggressor, why then does it continue? Instead of being intellectually justifiable, the selfish practitioner of sociobiology is merely the witless slave to his physical cravings which serve no useful purpose in the modern world. It is analogous to the plight of an overweight American who craves sweets. Before modern technology made sweets easily preserved and before our economy made sweets cheap, it made sense for people to consume sweets as soon as they were available. Today, the person who over-consumes is only hurting his health. In a similar fashion, our desires for political solutions to social problems are the byproducts of a selfish nature which may have been useful at some distant time in human history. Today, that selfish nature is killing us. This is my fourth point. Our selfish nature makes us want to oppress other people through politics, and we need to overcome that nature. This would be an impossible task since people cannot "step outside of their skin," but it is made possible by our adoption as Sons of God as a result of Christ's death and the Holy Spirit which now inhabits the bodies of every Christian believer.

I have already noted that all of the observed behavioral implications of evolution and sociobiology for people are also implied by the Bible. The Bible tells us that man is selfish but that he loves his own children (Mt 7:9, 10). The difference is that while the sociobiologist tells us that the selfish part of human nature is desirable, the Bible tells us that selfishness is a part of human nature which should be eliminated. Eph4:22–24 "That in reference to your former manner of life, you lay aside the old self, which

---

2. If this is a spiritual survival rather than a worldly survival, so much the better, because it is only our spirits which live forever. This world, and all of the things in it, must inevitably be destroyed. People agree that this is true whether they follow Christ or only the worldly astronomers. While our contemporary knowledge of the laws of astrophysics implies an inevitable destruction of the universe, spirit is not subject to the laws of this dimension and may survive eternally.

is being corrupted in accordance with the lusts of deceit and that you be renewed in the spirit of your mind and put on the new self which in the likeness of God has been created in the righteousness and holiness of the truth." As Christians, we are enabled to follow this advice and to overcome our natural desires to oppress other people. The sociobiologists' model of politics shows that politics is truly part of Satan's world. It is a world which Christians can and should avoid. We are left with no sound theory which says that political participation is good for Christians or even for the rest of mankind.

5

The Way of the World

"Be careful not to make a treaty with those who live in the land where you are going, or they will be a snare among you." (Ex 34:12)

CHRISTIANS ARE A "HOLY nation" (1Peter 2: 8–10). This holiness is something special which opens our relationship with our Creator and which enables us to be the light of the world. Association with things which are unholy can shade our light. Nonetheless, the world hates us (John 15:19), and it will make the worst of our associations whenever it is able to do so. Hence, even a fleeting association with evil can hurt our ability to witness.

I have already defined politics as the effort to re-write laws and explained that re-writing laws is a transfer of property. Consequently, some people seek to gain wealth from politics at the expense of others. This is just as true in a system of socialism as it is in a system of capitalism, since every known system of socialism has had inequality in enjoying the benefits of that system.

Just as the perpetrators of war have needed the bodies of Christians to fight for them and have seduced their souls to that end, the selfish manipulators of politics need the support of Christians and have deluded them into believing that they serve Christ through their efforts. Joining their efforts damages the witness of Christians and serves as a barrier against accepting Christ for the non-believers who are victims of politics.

One of the first times I ever worked as a professional economist was as the theoretician for the lobbyists hired to help Chrysler receive financing under favorable terms (in other words, a bailout) from the U.S. government in 1980. This was before I became a born-again Christian, and it is work which I would now refrain from doing. Nonetheless, as a graduate student seeking a PhD in Economics and Finance at the University of Southern California, I was offered this work and accepted it as I needed the money.

In 1980, Chrysler was on the brink of bankruptcy. There was substantial political support among the Congressmen from Michigan and other areas who had, among their constituents, many employees of Chrysler and its subcontractors pushing for a bailout of Chrysler. Nonetheless, Chrysler wanted the bailout to have an appearance of legitimacy. For that reason, they hired a team of economists to show that the arrangement was justified. My job was to create an economic theory which showed that since Chrysler was much smaller than its U.S. competitors (General Motors and Ford), the cost of regulatory compliance was a higher portion of Chrysler's revenues. As far as I could tell, none of the economists working on this team believed that the theory justified the bailout, but we completed the work for Chrysler and accepted our pay.

Similar lobbying is behind virtually every piece of important legislation which passes Congress. While most legislation is initiated by the parties who have the most to gain economically, in rare cases legislation is initiated by well-meaning persons who have nothing to gain. Either way, the final terms of the legislation are almost always dictated by the parties with the greatest financial stakes in its outcomes. This chapter will explain how this general outcome worked with three specific illustrations of legislation in the US: minimum wage legislation, the 1968 Gun Control Act, and the boycott of South Africa in the 1980s. All three of these illustrations involved laws which were supported by some well-intentioned Christians, but in all three cases those Christians were deceived.

Fair treatment to workers is a biblical principle (Lev 19:13, Jer 22:12–14, Malachi 3:5) as is charity to the poor (James 2: 5–6). With this background many Christians throughout the industrial world have supported legislation setting minimum wages. The US first passed laws setting minimum wages at the national level in 1938, and federal minimum wage legislation has been continuously in force since then.

Christian support for this legislation is misguided. First, our biblical instructions for fair treatment for workers and generosity to the poor are for us to follow individually. In no place does the Bible even suggest that we should force unbelievers to follow those instructions.

Economists have understood the theoretical effects of minimum wage legislation for at least a century. To the extent that minimum wage legislation sets a minimum wage that is higher than the wage where the quantity of labor supplied is equal to the quantity demanded, unemployment is a necessary result. More people will seek employment at the higher wage and fewer employers will find it profitable to hire workers at that wage. One way of re-stating "minimum wage" is that it is a law which prohibits employers from hiring people whose productivity is lower than the minimum rate. In light of this fairly simple logical result, why do legislators continuously set minimum wages? The answer is that, as with most economic legislation, the outcome is not even. Some people become poorer from minimum wage legislation, other people become richer, and sometimes there is no effect whatsoever.

The distributional effects of federal minimum wage legislation can best be illustrated by looking at a map which shows the states where Congressmen supported minimum wage and the states where Congressmen opposed minimum wage. In general, the Northeastern and industrial Middle Western states along with California supported minimum wage legislation. The South and most Western states opposed minimum wage.

The key characteristic which is common to all of the states which supported minimum wage is that the market wage rate in those states was already higher than the minimum wage. Consequently, few, if any people in those states were likely to lose their jobs. In cities like, Boston, New York, and San Francisco, very few workers earn only the Federal minimum wage anyway. Likewise, unionized workers are generally paid significantly more than minimum wage, so increases in minimum wage are not likely to affect their employment.

On the other hand, the Southern and Western states have many workers who earned wages below the new minimum immediately prior to each time the minimum was raised. Consequently, many of those workers became unemployed.

Now the question needs to be raised: who benefits from minimum wage? The answer is that the beneficiaries are the manufacturers and other employers in California, the Northeastern, and the industrial Middle Western states along with workers (particularly those who are unionized) in those same states. Minimum wage is an effective way of eliminating their competition from manufacturers and other businesses in the low-wage states. That is the real goal of minimum wage legislation. It is not some mistake of Congress. It is a concerted effort by one group to eliminate the competition from the other group. Many of the states which are opposed to minimum wage are "right to work" states in which labor unions have no effective power. If minimum wage legislation had not forced the

The Way of the World

manufacturers in those states to pay close to the same wages as were paid by manufacturers in Massachusetts, etc. then, the manufacturers in "right to work" states would have been able produce at a lower cost and ultimately drive the competition out of business.

Since it would be difficult for Congressmen to tell voters that they supported legislation designed to drive Southern and Western manufacturers out of business, other stories are created to support minimum wage. Just as I was paid to create a story which justified the federal government's bailout of Chrysler, economists are paid to find evidence which supports minimum wage. It is unfortunate that well-intentioned Christians are sometimes persuaded by these stories.

My second example of how legislation which seems to be the result of good intentions is driven by financial interests is the 1968 Gun Control Act. Christians are implored to peace, and violent crimes have plagued the U.S. since our founding. It is understandable that Christians would want to make it more difficult for people to obtain guns. Of course, we know that the only way to bring peace on earth is through Christ and leading people to follow Him. Nonetheless, many of the supporters of gun control have been Christians.

Violent crimes increased in the U.S. in the 1960's, and that was made particularly evident by the assassination of John F. Kennedy in 1963 and the assassinations of Martin Luther King, Jr. and Robert F. Kennedy in 1968. President Lyndon Johnson signed the 1968 Gun Control Act into law in October of that year, and it was followed by laws passed in several states prohibiting the sales of low-cost guns labeled Saturday Night Specials.

Most people are surprised to learn that the 1968 Gun Control Act and the laws prohibiting sales of Saturday Night Specials were supported by the major American gun manufacturers, principally Colt, Smith and Wesson, and Remington. That support, however, was not because they were good corporate citizens. In fact, those gun manufacturers were the principle beneficiaries of those pieces of legislation.

A rough summary of the major features of the 1968 Gun Control Act includes:

1. The prohibition of foreign-made firearms except for sporting purposes
2. The prohibition of mail-order sales of firearms
3. Requirements to mark guns with serial numbers
4. The prohibition of sales to certain felons

All of these features, except for the fourth, worked to reduce the competition to the major firearms manufacturers located in the Northeast of the U.S. The first feature stopped foreign manufacturers from competing with the U.S. firms for the military and police guns which were a large part of their business. Unlike foreign manufacturers and the newer manufacturers in the South and the West, all of the major Northeastern manufacturers had well-established networks of dealers through the U.S., and mail order was only a small part of their sales. Consequently, the second feature also reduced competition without hurting the marketing of the major gun makers in the Northeast. The major Northeastern manufacturers had all put serial numbers on their guns for many years, so the serial number requirement imposed a cost on their competition while not hurting them. While the fourth category could theoretically have hurt the sales of the Northeastern gun manufacturers, the categories of convicted felons who were prohibited from purchasing guns were so small in number as to not have any significant consequence for sales.

The state laws prohibiting "Saturday Night Specials" worked in a similar fashion. The established Northeastern gun manufacturers had old factories with expensive dies which were built to use steel with low zinc content. Newer gun manufacturers used lower-cost methods to make guns using steel with higher zinc content, and the legal definition of Saturday Night Special was based on zinc content and the melting point of the steel. That meant that the gun manufacturers based in the South and the West had to re-tool or shut down as states passed laws prohibiting Saturday Night Specials. As to the claim that Saturday Night Specials were used disproportionately in crime, reports of weapons confiscated from criminals by police departments in the U.S. showed that the confiscated weapons tended disproportionately to not be the Saturday Night Specials but the high-quality Colts, Smith and Wessons, and Remingtons which were manufactured in the Northeast. According to those police, most criminals took pride in the status of their weapons and, consequently, they did not buy the cheap guns made by the manufacturers in the South and the West. Those guns were primarily bought by low-income citizens seeking to protect themselves, and consequently many leaders of the black community in the U.S. were among the vocal protesters of the laws prohibiting Saturday Night Specials. Like the other gun control laws of that period, they had virtually nothing to do with controlling violence and were mostly aimed at controlling the competition of the Northeastern gun manufacturers.

The Way of the World

The politics behind the 1968 Gun Control Act bear an astonishing resemblance to the politics behind minimum wage legislation. Manufacturers in the Northeast were unable to successfully compete with the lower costs of manufacturers in the South and West as well as with manufacturers from abroad. Consequently, they supported laws to destroy the distribution systems of those manufacturers as well as to force them to incur unnecessary costs which the Northeastern manufacturers had already paid for their old factories. A map of the states where Congressmen supported or opposed gun control laws looks similar to the map which describes which states supported or opposed minimum wage legislation. It is roughly the same map which now describes the so-called Red (Republican) or Blue (Democrat) states. With this in mind, it is apparent that liberal versus conservative philosophies have nothing to do with the rift. It is about profits. In the Eastern half of the US, the same map describes the Union and the Confederacy during the US Civil War. That makes it clear why tariffs were a principle reason for the Southern states to try to leave the Union and for the Northern states to not want them to leave. The Northeastern manufacturers needed the South to buy their products, but they also needed tariffs since their costs were higher than manufacturing costs in England. That required that the South stay under U.S. law. Since no one would have been willing to fight and die to protect the profits of obsolete factories in Massachusetts, it was necessary to make it look like the war was about slavery. While his opposition to slavery was well-known, prior to the Civil War Abraham Lincoln had specifically stated that he had no intention to abolish slavery. In 1861 Lincoln even countermanded the orders of General John C. Fremont after Fremont ordered the freedom of slaves in Missouri, and he replaced Fremont when that general refused to cooperate with the reinstatement of slavery. Through this act Lincoln tried to show the South that he did not intend to abolish slavery. When it became necessary to obtain more political support for the war, however, Lincoln issued the Emancipation Proclamation freeing slaves in the rebel states. Christians from the North, who sought to "proclaim liberty throughout the land" (Lev 25:10) were among those who fought and died. It is difficult to believe that the same number of people would have joined the Union army if they had believed that the purpose of the war was to protect the profits of Northeastern manufacturers.

My third example in which financial interests usurped a good cause by writing a law in their own favor is the Comprehensive Anti-Apartheid Act which was passed in 1986. The stated purpose of this was to accelerate the end of apartheid in South Africa. The apostle Paul tells us that "There is no distinction between Jew and Greek" Romans 10:12. Consequently, Christians cannot condone any sort of discrimination based on race. In addition to the fact that Christians themselves should not discriminate, the demeaning nature of racial discrimination means that Christians should want to end it anywhere it exists. As with many of the issues which become politicized, however, the question is not whether we should seek this end. The question is how we should go about obtaining the desired result. Often the way of the world seems easier, but Christians who try that way inevitably lose. While Christ's way often seems like the hard way, we should remember Mt 11:30 "For my yoke is easy and my burden is light." Faith means that we act on Christ's words, even when something else appeals more to our senses.

The international movements to end apartheid in South Africa began in the late 1950's. Economic boycott of South Africa turned into a UN resolution in 1962, but the boycott was opposed by all Western nations. By 1968, however, Sweden's ambassador to the UN, Sverker Astrom, asked the Security Council to mandate economic sanctions against South Africa. Subsequently, political movements supporting the boycott increased in Western nations, culminating in the U.S. in the Comprehensive Anti-Apartheid Act of 1986 (CAAA).

The most important economic sanctions under the CAAA were prohibition of the import of (1) any gold coin minted in South Africa or sold by its Government, and (2) arms, ammunition, military vehicles, or any manufacturing data for such articles. Other economic provisions were in the act, such as prohibition of exporting computers to South Africa, but those provisions had exceptions which enabled people to get around them.

The prohibition of importing gold coins from South Africa had little in the way of economic consequences. Gold is a fungible commodity which can be easily melted and sold in international markets. Consequently, while Americans could not buy Krugerrands, much of the gold they bought in other forms came from South Africa, and gold from South Africa had the same price as gold from anywhere else. We were left then with the only important economic provision of the CAAA as the prohibition of importing military items from South Africa.

Why, then, did the economic consequences of this act center on the prohibition of imports of this one type of item? One might better answer that question by looking first at Sweden's efforts to create international sanctions against South Africa. Like South Africa, Sweden was a major exporter of military hardware. In essence, Sweden was eliminating a competitor in the international arms business. U.S. military manufacturers already had lobbies in Washington to influence Congress (as seen in the 1968 Gun Control Act). It was natural that those lobbies would draft legislation which stopped South African arms manufacturers from competing with them. Sweden is currently advocating boycotts of Israel, and it is probably no coincidence that, like South Africa and Sweden, Israel is a major exporter of military hardware.

In general, boycotts, whether legislated or done voluntarily, are not efficient ways of bringing about changes in behavior. Since a boycott means not trading with another party, the boycott hurts both the boycotter and the party being boycotted. The amount by which each is hurt depends on the shapes of the curves showing supply and demand, but under the most general assumptions of economics, the average boycotter is hurt as much as the average party being boycotted. The boycotter can usually choose to buy from someone else, just as the party being boycotted can choose to sell to someone else. On average, the loss to each is equal. Consequently, the average boycotter has costs of one dollar per each dollar lost by the party being boycotted. If the boycott is seeking to change behavior, the boycotter should then ask the question: is the best way to spend one dollar of my own resources to participate in a boycott which makes the other party poorer by one dollar? In general, the answer to that question is "no," and unless there is a spiritual violation from dealing with the boycotted party, the answer to a Christian is always "no."

We have better ways of changing behavior than by hurting or threatening to hurt other people. Witnessing for Christ is always our best way to change behavior. Since most of the white population of South Africa was at least nominally Christian in the 1960s, Christians should have witnessed about the fact that all races are equal in the eyes of the Lord. Since the boycott cost boycotters as much as it hurt the boycotted parties, Christians should have instead spent their money to directly help the black community in South Africa. They could, for example, have subsidized wages of black employees or built better housing for the black community. For the same cost, the beneficial effects of a direct subsidy would have almost certainly been better than any beneficial effects from the boycott.

The economic distribution of the effects from the embargo was perverse. While some white-owned manufacturing businesses (like military hardware) were hurt, the white-owned businesses which had the greatest exploitation of black labor (like gold mining) were helped. The embargo had no effect on the price at which South African gold miners were able to sell their gold. Gold is a fungible commodity which is easily smuggled. At the same time, the embargo resulted in a substantial decline in the value of the Rand (South Africa's currency). Since all of the costs of gold miners were in Rands while their sales were at the world price of gold, profit for gold miners increased as a result of the decline in value of the Rand. The embargo probably hurt black workers more than anyone else. As stated by Mangosuthu Buthelezi, Chief Minister of KwaZulu, and a leading black figure, "They can only harm all the people of Southern Africa. They can only lead to more hardships, particularly for the blacks."

Apartheid in South Africa officially ended in 1990, although the last vestiges of apartheid were not eliminated until the election of the African National Congress in 1994. It would be difficult to measure the extent to which ending that institution was due to embargo, internal violence, or just the gradual realization by South Africans that racial discrimination did not make sense. I personally believe that the last factor was the greatest, and that is consistent with my general observation that throughout history long-run changes in behavior only take place from changes in the spirituality and understanding of the participants. If that is the case, then increased witnessing by Christians would have been a more effective use of the resources which had been put into the embargo. In addition, behavior which changes as the result of changes in spirituality and understanding does not leave the resentment which sometimes lingers for generations following forced changes in behavior. Of course, it would have meant a few years of lower profits for Swedish and American arms manufacturers.

6

Taxation and Redistribution of Wealth

"Sell your possessions and give to charity; make yourselves money belts which do not wear out, an unfailing treasure in heaven, where no thief comes near nor moth destroys." (Luke 12:33)

CHARITY IS ONE OF the highest callings of Christians, and there are many references in both the Old and New Testaments to the fact that God is pleased with those who are charitable to the poor (Gal 2:10). The first gentile shown to be chosen for salvation was Cornelius, whose "prayers and alms had ascended as a memorial before God." At the same time, the rich receive repeated warnings about the possibility of their riches separating them from God (Luke 16: 19–23). It should not be surprising that Christian churches of most major denominations have at one time or another advocated that the rich be taxed at high rates in order to redistribute wealth to the poor. Today in the United States, inner-city churches with poor members of racial minorities sometimes support liberal Democrats who advocate wealth redistribution (while the suburban churches with affluent white members often support conservative Republicans who oppose wealth redistribution). This obvious conflict, and the fact that the Christians in each demographic group generally take the same positions as the non-Christians in their demographic group, should make it evident that the political issues are not Christian issues.

I have already noted that the effects of politics on economic activity are unobvious and not understood by most people. This is especially true in the area of taxation. Very few newspaper editors, accountants, or politicians have much understanding of the subject. I believe that understanding of

Christianity and Politics

the effects of legislation on economic activity is completely absent from the pastors of Christian churches with whom I have discussed these matters.

Taxes which are intended to produce "social justice" by redistributing the wealth of the rich to the poor seldom have the desired outcome. This is well illustrated by the popular story of Robin Hood. According to one version of this legend, Robin Hood lived in the forest outside of Nottingham, and would rob the rich merchants on their way in and out of the city. The loot would then be given to the poor. Whatever the truth or falsehood of this version of the legend, let us assume that this is what took place. Let us also assume that the merchants were based in big cities (like London), and that they chose the towns to which they would take their merchandise to sell based on economic considerations. Further assume that the people who bought merchandise in Nottingham and sold their produce there (townspeople, farmers, etc.) were unable to move to other locations.

After the first few months during which Robin Hood robbed the merchants, news of his activities would have disseminated throughout the community of merchants in big cities. Since the merchants were maximizers of their profits, they had previously taken goods to Nottingham as long as they earned at least as much profit from going to Nottingham as they would from going to any other town. Now they would consider the likelihood of being robbed by Robin Hood and the cost of the robbery, so many merchants would go to other towns instead of Nottingham. With fewer goods for sale in Nottingham, the price of those goods would rise. With fewer merchants buying farm produce, the price of farm produce would fall. This would mean that every merchant who successfully made the trip into and out of Nottingham without being robbed would earn an extraordinarily high profit. Those high profits would be offset by the risk and costs of sometimes being robbed by Robin Hood.

Merchants would only go to Nottingham when the expected profit, fully discounted for the risk of Robin Hood and, allowing for any required risk premium, was at least equal to the expected profit from going to other cities with their wares. Merchandise prices in Nottingham would be extraordinarily high and prices of farm produce would be extraordinarily low. Few transactions would take place, and Nottingham would become the most economically depressed region in England. Even if Robin Hood distributed everything he stole to the local farmers, keeping nothing for himself, due to the low quantities and the unfavorable prices, the farmers would be worse off than they were before Robin Hood began this program of "social justice." The merchants, however, would be roughly as well-off as they were before Robin Hood since most of them would go to other towns instead of Nottingham, and the few who continued going to Nottingham would occasionally reap extraordinary profits which sufficiently offset all of the costs from Robin Hood's plunder. Other than making his own name legendary, Robin Hood did no good for anyone.

The parable of Robin Hood is not too different from what actually occurs with taxes on the wealthy. Economic analysis tells us that the party who bears the economic burden of the tax does not need to be the same party as the one who physically pays a tax. In the case of the Robin Hood parable, the merchants paid the tax but bore none of the economic burden. The economic burden was instead borne by the farmers and townspeople whom Robin Hood intended to help.

The reasons for the unobvious result that robbing the traveling merchants does not hurt the traveling merchants but does hurt the townspeople and farmers are related to choices and alternatives. In this example, the merchants could choose between many different alternative towns to which to take their wares. The farmers and townspeople, however, were stuck in Nottingham, and had no choice. Economists describe the effects of these choices and alternatives in terms of elasticity. The essence for analysis of taxation is that the economic burden of a tax will be avoided by those who have many readily available choices, and that the economic burdens will wind up falling on the parties with fewer choices who transact with the parties who are directly taxed. (This result is rigorously derived in many elementary economics textbooks.) In our example, the traveling merchants had alternatives which enabled them to avoid the economic burden of the tax while the farmers and townspeople with whom they transacted had few alternatives.

For the most part the wealthy people of the world have many choices. If they derive their income from returns on their capital, they may be free to choose investments in any activity or in any part of the world. So many of the owners of capital have this freedom that the returns to capital, after taxes and after adjusting for risk, tend to be fairly equal throughout the world. If those risk-adjusted after-tax returns were not equalized, the wealthy who have the freedom to invest anywhere would simply invest less of their wealth in the activities and countries which have lower returns and more in the activities which have higher returns, until the returns were equal. It is the same adjustment process that the traveling merchants made when deciding to take their wares wherever the profits were highest, after adjusting for the possibility of being robbed. When a nation increases its rate of taxation on the returns to investment, investments flow out of that country and into other countries with lower rates of taxation. The force of human avarice is so great that these movements of capital can take place at a fairly rapid rate.

Working people with low skills probably have the least mobility and choices among the major groups of economic participants. They are often unable to move to different nations or regions within a nation, and even if they could move, the move would entail enormous emotional and economic costs. At the same time, those people are probably the greatest beneficiaries from capital flowing into their countries. Physical capital is machinery used for production, and that machinery makes workers more productive. Numerous economic studies confirm the fact that workers' wages rise as the amount of capital in a nation increases. The importance of capital to workers at the lowest rung of the economic ladder is illustrated by the fact that nations which have very little capital per worker (such as most of sub-Saharan Africa) have typical wages of about $300 per year for workers at the lowest rung of the economic ladder, while those wages would typically run about $15,000 or more per year in the U.S. or Western Europe. This relative difference (about fifty to one) is much more than the relative difference in the wages of more skilled workers (such as computer programmers or engineers).

When a nation increases its rates of taxation on the owners of capital, those owners send their capital abroad, where it can earn returns which are often unreported to the nation of origin. Since this reduces the amount of available machinery which helps workers to produce, the workers become less productive and their wages decline. Nations which tax the owners of capital at high rates, therefore, tend to have great disparity between the standards of living of the rich and the working class. They are also poor nations without a great deal of tax revenue which winds up being paid to their governments. It is no coincidence that the nations which have the best combination of political stability and low taxes on capital (probably Switzerland and the U.S.), have the most capital per worker and the highest overall standards of living.

The effects of taxing the incomes of highly skilled workers at high rates are similar but less dramatic. Those workers probably have more mobility than the poor, but less mobility than the owners of capital. The poor benefit from the services of the highly skilled workers, so they bear some cost from this type of tax. That cost is still less than the cost to the poor from the loss of capital in their own locality.

Since these results are fairly well established in economic theory, why do politicians try to tax the returns to capital at high rates? There are a variety of reasons for this. Partially it is out of ignorance. It is also done to make a nice show for the voters. The effects which I have described require some time to take place. It takes time for the capital which is located in a nation to be moved or to deteriorate and be replaced elsewhere. While these time periods (probably an average of around seven years for manufacturing equipment to lose half of its value) are relatively short by the standards of world history, they may be long relative to the expected tenure of a politician. The immediate effect of high taxes is often high revenue because the taxpayers have not yet moved or changed their activities. This high revenue is often helpful to the politicians who have short-run incentives.

The other side of political wealth redistribution to produce social justice is equally destructive. In essence, the politicians make some definition of the class of citizen which they believe is deserving of more income, and the government makes payments to that group. Simple economic analysis would tell us that whatever the definition is for that group, payments to people who meet that definition over a long period of time will mean that we wind up with more people in that group. In the 1960s in the U.S., Aid to Families with Dependent Children (AFDC) was created to make payments to families which had children but no working adult. Over the next twenty years, the number of children in families with no working adult exploded. Did this take place through more fatal injuries or disabilities among the adults? No. The statistics indicate that the principal growth in the number of dependent children was through illegitimate birth. The rate of illegitimate births (as a percentage of all births) went from 11 percent in 1970 to 28 percent in 1990. Any decent economist could have predicted this result simply by reading the rules for qualifying for AFDC. Similarly, any decent sociologist should have been able to predict that an explosion in the rate of illegitimate births would have effect years later of more teenagers belonging to criminal gangs and a surge in the rate of violent crime. The problem was not with the desire to help the poor, but that rules which define need for welfare encourage people to meet the definition of being needy.

The end results of political attempts to redistribute wealth have been: First, less productive activity by the wealthy, second, less productive activity by the poor, third, deterioration in the moral standards of the poor and fourth, resentment by the wealthy and the middle class. These end results can be contrasted with the results of true Christian charity. No Christian resents his freely given offerings for the Lord's work. Instead of avoiding the receipt of income, Christians often seek more income purely for the purpose of being able to give more to Christian charity. At the same time, one seldom hears of the recipients of Christian charity behaving immorally to qualify for more money. When the recipients are the members of a small local church which has made anonymous donations to a collection for Christian works, those recipients are universally grateful, and their love for fellow Christians is increased. The love of the donors is also increased as they see their donations helping their brethren. Non-Christian recipients of Christian charity may have their own hearts opened by the kindness of Christians, and it is certainly the case that there is, on average, better supervision of the worthiness of the recipients than with a government program.

Does the inability of political programs for wealth redistribution to produce many good results mean that Christians should campaign against these programs? No, because reducing taxes on the wealthy is not a Christian issue. It is an issue of good government but, as with other issues which are not purely Christian, we will be misled and ultimately make ourselves bad examples by these efforts. The final wording of most legislation in the area of taxation tends to be influenced by parties with narrow selfish interests, and political campaigning by Christians for tax reform would make the world believe that we are associated with those narrow selfish interests, either as their allies or as their dupes. *Newsweek* magazine recently mocked Christian organizations involved in these campaigns, stating that Jesus had no position on the issue of capital gains taxation. The remark was valid. Let us not set ourselves up for the derision of the world.

7

How to Change Behavior

"Or how can you say to your brother, 'Let me take the speck out of your eye,' and behold, the log is in your own eye?" (Mt 7:4)

ULTIMATELY, CHRISTIANS IN POLITICS intend to change the behavior of other people, both believers and non-believers. With both groups, Christian political efforts are doomed to failure because we are attempting to change behavior without changing motivation. Legislation requiring Christian behavior is particularly dangerous because it can make people appear to behave as Christians when they do not know or love Christ. It dilutes Christ's message and it makes witnessing more difficult. This is one of the biggest dangers of Christian involvement in politics. As Martin Luther said,[1] "I say it a hundred thousand times, God will have no forced servitude."

The basis of Christianity is not behavior; it is a loving relationship with God, through his Son Jesus. This love is reflected in our feelings and manifested in our behavior. Through God's word, the Bible, we learn what types of behavior are pleasing to God and what types of behavior are not pleasing, but it is our love and pure feelings which are truly pleasing to Him. Christ's Sermon on the Mount tells us that bad desires in our heart are just as bad as bad behavior. God wants holy people who love him, and when such people are properly instructed they will not have bad behavior. Evil comes from the hearts of men. (Mt 16:19)

A major message of the Bible is that God does not merely want the act of obedience. God wants our love. All commandments follow from the

---

1. Broadbent 147.

Great Commandment to love God with all of our heart, soul, and might and the corollary commandment to love our neighbor as we love ourselves. Obedience to God is a sign of our love for him and our neighbor, and that is the greatest importance of obedience.

God could force us to obey at anytime; that would be a very easy task for him. What God wants instead is very difficult. What God wants is so difficult that it is the one goal which has a great cost, even for God. He wants created beings with a free will to love him and to obey him because of that love. He wants to have a perfect relationship with us, but a perfect relationship with created beings who are endowed with free-will is obstructed by our sin and the hardness of our hearts. Divine purity and spirit had to be imparted to these created beings, and the only way that this could be achieved was through the sacrifice of God's only begotten Son, Jesus. Jesus even asked the Father if there was another way. There was none. The task fell on Jesus. When we use worldly means to get non-believers to behave as Christians, we turn our backs on Christ's sacrifice. Using worldly methods to force Christian behavior degrades the great price which God paid in his effort to bring us into a relationship with him.

The value of the relationship which God seeks with man can be understood best through observing family relationships. A parent may ask a child to obey, but the child's obedience means very little if it comes only from the fear of punishment. Obedience out of love, however, can bring great joy to both child and parent. It moves both family members closer to a perfect relationship. As anyone with children knows, however, this sort of obedience and this sort of relationship is as difficult to achieve as it is valuable.

Imagine a situation in which a wealthy man has adopted a child from an orphanage in an impoverished nation. Due to years of abuse in the orphanage, the orphan is unresponsive to the man's love. The man would so much like the orphan to run up and hug him when he gets home from work. The man's older child knows about her father's desire to have the child hug him, so she slaps the child on the face, telling the child that there will be more punishment if the child does not hug the father when he returns from work that day. Will the man be happy with the older child? Certainly not, since the effect of the slapping will be only to push the adopted child farther from the father.

Just as the wealthy man would not be happy with the older child who slaps the adopted child to produce the appearance of love, so our Father in Heaven cannot be happy with Christians who force non-believers to obey him out of fear of punishment on earth. In this case, the cost to the Father to win the love of the child was the loss of his Only Begotten Son. That makes the relationship all the more important, and mere acts of obedience will not satisfy. Using this analogy, it is unChristian to try to force unbelievers to obey God.

Would it be more pleasing to God if non-believers with wicked hearts behaved better? I cannot find any firm biblical basis for this. God destroyed the world in the Great Flood because man was wicked and "every intent of the thoughts of his heart was only evil continually" (Gen: 6:5). The men of Sodom were destroyed because they were wicked, and their outcry had become so great (Gen 19:20), but the wickedness (as contrasted with righteousness) was a characteristic of the men of Sodom, and that characteristic was manifested in bad behavior. It is not clear if God would have treated Sodom differently if these wicked men with evil intentions had been forced to behave better. As Paul states in Romans 1:28, "Therefore, since they did not think it worthwhile to retain the knowledge of God, he gave them over to a depraved mind, to do what ought not to be done." In other words, God gave men over to sinful behavior as a consequence of their not knowing him. This seems to indicate that it is not God's will that we stop the sinful behavior in other people without bringing them to know Him. Similarly, prayers and worship from non-believers are only a mockery, so this kind of "better behavior" does not please Him.

Christ lists six commandments, however, which must be kept for eternal life (Mt 19:18–19). We know from these and other Scriptures that behavior of believers matters to God. As Paul states "What business is it of mine to judge those outside the church? Are you not to judge the behavior of those inside?" (1Cor 5:12) If it is only the behavior of believers that should matter to us, however, all of the efforts of Christians in politics are futile since we would be pursuing an end which is irrelevant. The Bible gives clear advice to the Church concerning how we should improve the behavior of believers, and the advice does not require the force of government.

There are a few possibilities which could make the behavior of non-believers relevant. One possibility is that because non-believers may someday be saved, their souls would be then preserved for eternity. It may matter that those souls would have less that must be destroyed by the fire of God in our ultimate perfection (1Cor 3:15). My understanding, however, is that this is a destruction of wicked feelings rather than some destruction caused by wicked deeds. A second possibility might be derived from Luke

12:47–48 in which the Lord describes that there will be fewer stripes applied to those who did not know that they violated the law. If these verses are for the unsaved, then it is an indication that there are varying degrees of punishments for their sins, and we may be saving them "stripes" by keeping them from sin. Alternatively, even if these verses are for the unsaved, they may only be dividing sinners into two groups, one which knows the will of the Lord and another that sins without knowing. Since these verses refer to a steward and slaves of the master, it is most likely that they are intended for the saved, and they do not say anything about the importance of the behavior of the unsaved.

A third possibility is that knowledge of their own sinful actions may create a barrier between unbelievers and God which hinders salvation. This argument has problems, however, since Christ came for sinners. It reverses the causality already quoted in Romans 1: 24–30 and a main theme of the Gospel that the knowledge of God, through his Son Jesus Christ, is the only way to overcome sin. We know that no one can completely obey the Law, and therefore every person must be saved by the sacrifice of Jesus Christ, and not his own deeds. Those who have much to repent will be more joyful upon hearing of the good news of their salvation. (Luke 7:47) The Pharisees (whose sins were less evident to the people around them) were more reluctant to receive Jesus as their Savior than were the overt sinners. Therefore, the lack of sins which are evident to those around us (while retaining the sins of our feelings) may be a greater barrier to salvation than overt and highly visible sin.

A fourth possibility is that the wicked actions of the unsaved hinder the spiritual development of the saved. I know of no biblical verses which would support this, however. This book is not dealing with the overt actions which illegally damage another party under current law in the U.S. (such as rape, assault, etc.). The damage to the souls of the saved from the wicked (but legal) behavior of the unsaved is therefore limited to the unsaved being bad examples. Since the behavior of the unsaved is a contrast rather than an example to Christians, however, this fourth possibility is a fairly weak one.

In the final analysis, there is not much of a biblical basis for changing the behavior of the unsaved without changing their hearts. Since I do not pretend, however, to have the correct interpretation of the entire Bible, or to understand all of God's heart, I will assume that there is a reason to change behavior of the unsaved without changing their hearts and that I simply do not understand that reason. The rest of my analysis will rely on that assumption.

How to Change Behavior

My principal point in the rest of this chapter is that even if we want to change behavior, legislation is a poor way to do this as compared with the alternatives of evangelism, prayer, charity, and being good examples. Legislation will result in behavioral changes which are small relative to what can be made by evangelism, it will harden the hearts of the unsaved, and it will require Christians to make compromising and corrupt alliances. Rather than spend our energy to change legislation, we should spend that same energy to change hearts.

First of all we must remember that legislation seldom changes behavior if there is no enforcement. In order for legislation to have any real effect, it is necessary that the violations be detected, that the violators be apprehended, that they be convicted in court, and that a suitable punishment is carried out. Academic studies on the effects of punishment on crime have shown that it is only when all four steps are completed that legislation has any real effect. If even one of the four steps is neglected, then the legislation is unlikely to affect behavior.

Because of the difficulty of taking all four of these steps, legislation prohibiting some behavior is impractical. For example, the U.S. passed legislation (a Constitutional Amendment) which prohibited the sale and consumption of alcoholic beverages and this was enforced under the Volstead Act from 1919–1936. Alcohol is easily manufactured from commonly available foodstuffs and grains. Since alcohol was legal in most of the rest of the world, it was easy to obtain outside of the U.S. borders. For those reasons, it was difficult to detect if someone made alcohol or even if they brought it into the U.S. from Canada or Mexico. Because large parts of the U.S. population did not support the Volstead Act in their hearts, it was easy for violators to find allies who would help them to not be apprehended. Prosecuting attorneys also found it difficult to win convictions, and the punishments which were actually meted out were not sufficient to provide a deterrent. We were left with laws which were widely ignored and which introduced many Americans to criminal activity. It is generally recognized that the legislation was a failure and that it helped organized crime in America.

Part of the problem with the enforcement of Prohibition was that there were no identifiable victims who wanted to bring their case to court. This is very different from laws which prohibit theft or assault in which case there are victims who want the laws enforced. All of the behavioral legislation which is discussed in this chapter is of the first type. There are no identifiable victims who are able to bring charges against the violator to the legal system. That makes this legislation difficult to enforce. The U.S. Supreme Court's decisions have been consistent with this difficulty of enforcement when the Court has ruled that the government has no authority over the private acts of individuals.

Probably the most sensitive political issue for most Christians in the U.S. in the 1990s has been the legality of abortion. In 1973 the U.S. Supreme Court ruled that a fetus in the first trimester was not a legal person, and that the right to privacy gave women and their physicians the right to perform abortions during the first three months of pregnancy. The number of abortions in the U.S. was approximately 1.2 million in 1994, the most recent year for which data is available. The rate of abortions reached a high of 377 per 1000 live births in 1981 and has fallen since then to the current rate of about 280 abortions per 1000 live births. Since most abortions were previously illegal we do not have accurate figures on the number of abortions performed prior to 1973. The highest estimate I have read is 1,000,000 abortions per year in the late 1940s, while the lowest estimate I have read is 130,000 abortions per year in the late 1960s.

While the Bible does not directly discuss abortion, virtually all Christians agree that most (if not all) of the abortions which take place are immoral acts. Disagreements among Christians concerning the immorality of abortion are mostly limited to the cases where the mother was a victim of rape or where the mother's life is endangered. Since those cases constitute less than 2 percent of all abortions in the U.S. I will ignore them and assume that Christians agree that abortion is immoral.

Clearly, the fetus suffers during an abortion. Nonetheless, most evangelical Christians who have thought about the subject would agree that the real victim of an abortion is the woman who chooses the abortion. That woman's soul is damaged. There is no damage to the soul of the baby that is killed. God is just and gives those children at least as much opportunity as is given to any other unsaved person who dies with no exposure to the Gospel (Ps 33:5).

The nature of abortion fits the type of behavior discussed in this chapter due to the fact that there are no parties with legal standing who have an incentive to sue. Courts have determined that the father of an aborted baby has no standing, and, of course, the baby itself is left unable to sue. Whether the courts have erred is not a matter of Christianity. The federal government is legally obligated to comply with decisions of the U.S. Supreme Court. Those decisions are made to comply with judges' understandings

How to Change Behavior

of historical rights and laws, and they will sometimes be inconsistent with Christian doctrine. If the justices of the Supreme Court are honest men, they must follow their legal analysis even if it leads to interpretations which have implications which are unfavorable for Christians. That is not a reason for Christians to oppose the decisions, although it may be a reason why serving as a member of the Supreme Court would violate the conscience of some Christians.

Christians who are justifiably disturbed over abortion must pray for guidance and read the Word of the Lord to determine how to direct their efforts. Our ultimate question is "What would Jesus do?" The way of the world is to choose a political solution. That entails passing laws to detect, prosecute, and punish abortionists and women who have abortions. I believe that Jesus would choose prayer and evangelism. There is no biblical basis for anything else.

Does the way of the world work better than the way of Jesus? We know that it cannot, and I believe that careful analysis confirms this.

First of all, in order to make abortion illegal in the face of a Supreme Court decision which grants abortion on demand in the first trimester, it would require a constitutional amendment which must be ratified by three-quarters of the states. This would be virtually impossible without an overwhelming popular support. The hearts of many people would need to be changed just to pass the appropriate legislation.

That would not end abortion, however. It would be necessary for the legislation to make provisions for detection of violators and punishment. Since the nature of abortion is that it can take place without anyone who opposes the abortion knowing, detection may be difficult. This is especially so due to the facts that an abortion inducing drug, RU-486, is widely available in Europe, and home abortion kits are likely to soon be available. The drug RU-486 requires two doses separated by a twelve day period. It normally also requires the observations of a physician, but persons using the drug illegally would probably be willing to forfeit the safety associated with a physician's observation. Illegal drugs of other sorts are widely available in the U.S. at mark-ups which average less than $5.00 per pill so a reasonable expectation is that drugs producing abortion would be available even if they were illegal. An abortion which was illegally performed through RU-486 or a home kit would be virtually impossible to detect. Essentially, the only results of making abortions illegal would be to raise the cost of abortion very slightly and to increase the associated medical dangers.

As already noted, we do not know how many abortions took place in the U.S. when abortions were illegal. However many that may be, it is likely that if abortions were made illegal today, the number of illegal abortions performed would be greater than it was in the past. This is due to both changed technology which would make an abortion at home easier, and due to the changed hearts of millions of American women who view abortion as a woman's right. In fact, illegality which was brought about by the efforts of Christians may further harden the hearts of those women. We would have taken legal rights which those women now possess and transferred them to ourselves.

A study of the international statistics on abortion can give some light on the effects of legality. I want to be very careful introducing statistics, however, since I know that the interpretation of statistics is fraught with potential for error. I also know that when people interpreting statistics have emotions and other interests in making a particular interpretation, they will tend to make the interpretation which best suits their interest. I will try to avoid any misinterpretation and ask the reader to do the same. While there is a possible loss of predictive power, I have tried to make my statistics as simple as possible so that they can be easily reproduced by readers.

The abortion rate varies widely among countries whose laws permit abortion on demand. If we describe the abortion rate as the number of known abortions per 100 pregnancies (which count births, abortions, and miscarriages) the abortion rate in the U.S. is 29.7. In other words, 29.7 percent of pregnancies in the U.S. end in abortion. The world's highest abortion rate is in the former Soviet Union where it was estimated to be between 55 and 68. The most liberal abortion laws in Western Europe are probably those of the Netherlands, however, and the abortion rate in the Netherlands is only 9.0. Belgium and Ireland have the strictest abortion laws in Western Europe, permitting abortion only to save the mother's life, and their abortion rates are 8.7 and 5.9 respectively, although the Belgian rate rises to 12.2 when it includes women who go abroad (often to the Netherlands) for their abortions. All abortions are illegal in Mexico, but based on the widely-quoted estimate that there are 1,500,000 abortions per year in Mexico (140,000 Mexican women die each year from the complications of abortion); the Mexican abortion rate is approximately 27.

On the whole, nations which have legalized abortion have much higher rates than nations in which abortion is illegal. For the three nations with reported statistics which permitted abortion only to save the mother's life, the unweighted average abortion rate was 7.7. The 7.7 statistic is probably a low estimate, however, since it only includes legal abortions, and countries which permit abortion only to save the mother's life probably have more illegal abortions than countries which grant abortion on demand. The rate rises to 12.5 by including Mexico (which outlaws all abortions) in the sample.

For the nineteen nations with reported statistics which permitted abortion on demand the unweighted average rate was 29.1, about the same as the U.S. rate. By comparison, the mean abortion rate in countries which allow abortion only to save the mother's life is about 43 percent of the mean abortion rate in countries which allow abortion on demand. The portion of this difference in the two means which can be attributed purely to legal differences is reduced, however, by the fact that laws generally reflect public views. The abortion rate of Ireland would be very unlikely to rise to the rate of the Soviet Union even if abortions were made legal on demand in Ireland. By the same token, it is very unlikely that the abortion rate in the Soviet Union could fall to the abortion rate in Ireland simply by abortions being made illegal. My best guess is that even if Ireland legalized abortion on demand, Ireland would still have one of the lowest abortion rates in the world, and even if the former Soviet Union made all abortions illegal, it would still have the highest rate.

The greatest difference between abortion rates is the difference between countries, even when those countries have the same legal status for abortion. The abortion rate in the former Soviet Union, for example, is more than 6 times the abortion rate in the Netherlands even though both countries permit abortion on demand. The abortion rate in Mexico (where all abortions are illegal) is higher than the rate in four of the five reporting Western European countries which grant abortion on demand. Something besides the law has a major effect on the abortion rate. It is not just economic; the U.S. abortion rate is more than twice the abortion rate in Vietnam even though Vietnam has abortion on demand and the per capita income in Vietnam is less than 5 percent of the per capita income in the U.S. The availability of birth control cannot explain this difference either, since birth control is more readily available in the U.S. than it is in Vietnam. I can conclude only that the difference is the hearts of people. The point is that a change in the law without a change in people's hearts will have some effect on behavior, but the magnitude of the change in behavior is small compared with the magnitude which can come by changing hearts.

What can Christians do to reduce the abortion rate? We can pray and witness. We can make kind offers to expectant mothers to provide them with living arrangements, provide for their medical care, and, if they so desire, to adopt their unwanted children. Christians in the U.S. are already doing these things, and they are working. The abortion rate in the U.S. has fallen by more than 25 percent since 1983 with no new legal restrictions on abortion. To the extent that the decline in the abortion rate can be attributed to Christian efforts, then those Christians may have prevented over 400,000 abortions per year.

Our job here is far from complete. We can offer still more in living expenses, medical care and adoption opportunities to women who bear their unwanted children. We must try to have a loving family available to adopt each and every child, regardless of the child's race or birth defects. We must make it known that we are doing this and that we are doing it out of love. We must be good witnesses. This is not an easy job, but it has shown success so far. I see very little hope of making abortion illegal in the U.S., and if it is made illegal I doubt that it would reduce the abortion rate by as much as the drop between 1983 and 1996.

The most difficult thing that Christians can do to help the abortion problem is to be good examples. It is difficult because it requires changing our own behavior and it requires that we do it each and every day. The potential effects of this, however, are enormous. Of the 1.2 million abortions which took place in the U.S. in 1994, only 18.4 percent were performed on married women not separated from their husbands. Putting this another way, at least 80 percent of the U.S. abortion problem is due to lack of respect for the institution of marriage.

Sexual immorality includes all sexual relations outside of marriage. It is destructive to our relationships with our spouses, and it is destructive to our souls. The institution of marriage is an earthly model for the Church's relationship with Christ, and adultery is a violation of our relationship with God. Prayer and witnessing can help to end sexual immorality, but there is a great need for Christians to be good examples. About 18 percent of abortions were performed on women who identified themselves as born-again or evangelical Christians.

The divorce rate in the U.S. is highly correlated with the abortion rate. The annual rate of divorces in the U.S. approximately tripled between 1965 and 1983. Since 1983 it has fallen by about 20 percent. The pattern is virtually identical to the pattern for the abortion rate. This would lead a statistician to suspect that abortion and divorce had common causes.

While the rise in divorce rates can be partially attributed to no-fault divorce laws in many states, there is another side. We must blame ourselves. The position of Christian churches in the U.S. has taken a dramatic turn in the past 30 years for permitting divorce. Thirty years ago, it would have been difficult for someone to find a fundamentalist Christian church which permitted a divorced person to re-marry. In 1997 it is very difficult to find any Christian church which will not permit a divorced person to re-marry. It is very difficult in 1997 to find any Christian church which will not permit a divorced and re-married man to become an elder. If there is a difference between the national divorce rate and the divorce rate among most denominations of fundamentalist Christians, it is not so large that I can determine it exists from the small sample of my own observations. According to *Newsweek* [2] 70 percent of Southern Baptist pastors report counseling women who have committed fornication with other pastors, and the divorce rate among Protestant clergy is approximately the same as the divorce rate among the general population. Jesus tells us to not try to remove the speck from another person's eye when we have a log in our own eye. Divorce is the log in the eye of the Christian community in the United States, and it has an effect on the rate of abortions in the US.

My personal observation is that among fundamentalist churches in Southern Orange County, California, *fornication* is winked at. When it involves a church leader, it is sometimes kept hidden and, under the guise of forgiveness, the violator might not lose his place of leadership. Jesus' position on divorce is quite clear. In fact, divorce is the single area of scriptures in which Christ's position is most often repeated, a fact which emphasizes the importance of the subject. Matthew 5:32 states that anyone who divorces his wife except for unchastity makes her commit adultery. It also states that anyone who marries a woman who is divorced (no exceptions are given) commits adultery. Mark 10:11–12 tells us that whoever divorces his or her spouse and marries another commits adultery (no exceptions are given for this as well). Using Jesus Christ's definitions, adultery was very common in fundamentalist Christian churches in 1997. It should be noted that while Jesus clearly spoke against both divorce and re-marriage following a divorce, there are cases in which separation is necessary (1Cor 7:15). Interpreting this to condone divorce, however, is inconsistent with the preponderance of scriptures on this subject, and must therefore be an incorrect interpretation.

2. *Newsweek* (7/28/1997), 62.

Christianity and Politics

As with most other questions of personal behavior, Christians should ask themselves "What would Jesus do?" When I discuss with other Christians my views on the need of Christians to avoid violence, the other Christians sometimes bring out the relatively violent acts of Jesus when he scourged the Temple of the money changers. As always Jesus was a good example, but his example must be carefully interpreted. Jesus' scourging of the temple was not to punish the sinners of the world. Jesus came to save sinners and showed them mercy in all occasions. Jesus cleansed the Temple (John 2:16) in fulfillment of the prophecy that "Zeal for My House will Consume Thee" (Psalms 69:9). He then proceeded through analogy to show that the Body of Christ was the Temple. Christ's treatment of His Church has a different standard than the treatment given to unbelievers. The Church represents souls which have been forgiven and Saved for Eternity. As Paul notes (I Cor 5:5), the best way to show love for wayward Christians is sometimes a harsh treatment which cleanses their souls.

In order to follow Jesus' example of scourging the Temple, we must cleanse the Body of Christ. We should start with the leadership of our churches. If our leaders do not meet the requirements set in I Timothy 3, they should be asked to resign. Divorce while holding a leadership position would indicate that the leader could not manage his own house well. Divorce and remarriage would make the leader the husband of more than one wife. This is not punishment, and it is not mere obedience to the Law. It is only following scriptural advice for management of the church. This means that the approximately 50 percent of Protestant clergy who are divorced must lose their jobs and find other work if they either initiated the divorce or re-married.

We must also do something about the high divorce rate among the rest of the Church. I have recently come to believe that this is also a problem which can be solved by biblical understanding and adherence of our elders and pastors. Some Christian assemblies still follow literal interpretation of the Bible with regard to marriage and refuse to marry people who have divorced their spouses. While my statistics on those assemblies are not from large samples and have been assembled in an ad hoc manner, they indicate that of all marriages performed by those assemblies, only about 1 percent end in divorce. The 1 percent figure is so far below the mean of all Christian assemblies, that it leads me to believe that a concerted effort to follow biblical instructions on marriage leads to a substantial reduction in the divorce rate.

Other segments of the U.S. society also have low divorce rates, indicating that the U.S.'s liberal divorce laws are not the cause of widespread divorce. Mexican immigrants to the U.S., for example, have a divorce rate which is approximately one tenth of the divorce rate of the population at large (Wall Street Journal November 18, 1998). Christian churches in the United States have no excuse for divorce rates which are similar to those of unbelievers. While stricter laws on divorce may be a matter of good government, enactment of those laws is not a Christian issue. Christians are called to higher standards than the rest of the world, and our high standards on marriage can be enforced by church leaders.

Should annulment of marriage be permitted? While there is no biblical basis of annulment it stands to reason that in cases of genuine coercion (such as a gun pointed at the head of the bride or groom) no valid marriage has taken place. Similar analysis can be applied to genuine immaturity of the bride or groom. In either case, however, an annulment based on the grounds that the marriage could not have been valid indicates that the church leader performing the marriage service had been negligent and that his negligence caused great harm to several people. Negligence in the Church function of marriage is grounds for removal from office under I Timothy 3. If a church were to simply defrock any person who performed a marriage ceremony which later resulted in annulment, I have little doubt that it would bring about a drastic reduction in the number of annulments allowed by that church. Anything less than this is a mockery of the marital institution, and the unbelieving world is clearly aware of the present mockery of marriage by Christian churches.

Am I saying that if Christian churches refused to perform marriages which amounted to adultery under Christ's definition that the divorce rate would fall? Yes, and I doubt that anyone who thinks about this issue would question that conclusion. The Christian divorce rate has risen in tandem with the general divorce rate in the U.S. over the past thirty years. Showing a biblical regard for the sanctity of marriage can lower the divorce rate within our churches. This means that neither a divorced woman nor a man who has divorced his wife may remarry in a Christian church while their spouse is still living. (Luke 16:18)

I am also saying that if Christian churches refused to perform marriages which constituted adultery that the abortion rate would fall! I have already noted that at least 80 percent of abortions in the U.S. can be attributed to lack of regard for the institution of marriage. When I talk about the institution of marriage with unbelievers who fornicate, I often hear answers indicating that they believe marriage does not mean anything today. They only need to look inside most Christian churches to see this. The world of unbelievers closely watches the behavior of the Christian community, and we need to become a good example in the marital institution. Setting that example can reduce sexual immorality and subsequently reduce the abortion rate. Abortions are highly correlated with the divorce rate. While statistics cannot show causal relationships, they are often an indication that one exists. In fact, I believe that a return to sanctity of the marital relationship within the Christian church would reduce the abortion rate by a much larger amount than it could ever be reduced by legislation!

Attempts to reduce the abortion rate by legislation have been a failure. Good examples and biblical church policies can clearly reduce the divorce rate. If the good examples of Christian marriage reduce fornication, those same good examples may contribute to a significant reduction in the abortion rate. Since the divorce rate among lay couples and Protestant clergy approximately matches the average of unbelievers, the Christian community in the United States in the twentieth century has been a failure in this area.

The Christian who wants to reduce the abortion rate will certainly do more good by spending time witnessing, praying, and acting as a good example than through legislation. Trying to change legislation may seem to be the practical way to reduce abortion, but it is not. Legislation is unlikely to pass and behavior is unlikely to change without first changing people's hearts. When their hearts are changed, people will want to follow Christ in abortion and also in all other areas. Furthermore, by witnessing and praying the Christian is following the commandments of our Lord Jesus Christ and coming closer to Him.

A proper respect by Christian churches for the sanctity of marriage will help other areas of behavior as well. A recent study reported that 66 percent of inmates in California prisons had been in foster care, at least at sometime during their childhoods.[3] It is evident from this that the vast majority of crime is committed by people who did not grow up with a traditional household of two loving parents. Reduction of divorce within the Christian church is almost certain to reduce crime in general.

The solution to other problems of behavior which are unChristian is the same as the solution to the problem of abortion. Prayer, evangelism and setting good examples are more effective than any political efforts.

3 Orange County Register (10/25/2004).

How to Change Behavior

Sodomy is offensive to God, to Christians, and to most unbelievers, but do we honestly believe that making it illegal will cause it to stop? Even more important, can we expect illegality to make any change in the hearts of people who have perverted sexual lusts? Regardless of what legislation could be passed, the problems of detection and enforcement are untenable. I doubt that legislation has ever changed the perverted sexual desires of any person, but the Holy Spirit has changed the souls of millions. Our behavior as Christians can help this process.

I recently witnessed to a practicing homosexual unbeliever who was familiar with the Gospel. He asked me whether my church would treat heterosexual fornication and adultery with the same condemnation as was given to homosexual acts. The unbeliever noted that Jesus never condemned sodomy, per se, but only by implication through his condemnation of adultery and fornication, so it was hypocrisy to condemn sodomy if heterosexual fornication is ignored. The unbelieving sodomite was right. If we tolerate fornication and adultery in the Church, then we have no credibility when we witness to the world.

The condemnation by Christians of homosexual behavior among unbelievers is often a hypocritical manifestation of our natural (Darwinian) feelings which we attempt to cover with the shroud of morality. Nazis, fascists, and other worldly political factions which sometimes garner Christian support have used our natural feelings of hostility toward homosexuals for their own causes. When we join them, the world associates all of their offenses with the Body of Christ, and it makes our real goal of leading souls to Christ more difficult. We can best facilitate our goals by making ourselves holy and loving examples.

The basic elements of Godly behavior are legislated and enforced throughout the one-fifth of the world which is Islamic. In those nations, sodomy and adultery can bring the penalty of death. There is no drunkenness, no pornography, and no public blasphemy of God's name. The absence of those behaviors has not brought Muslims closer to God. In fact, due to these strict moral prohibitions, the need for Christ is less evident to the billion unbelievers who live in those nations. Christians have the high calling of bringing people into a relationship with God. When we leave this role to try to force the behavior of non-believers, then we have abandoned our duty to Christ.

The Bible tells us that Christians are a peculiar people, set apart for the Lord (Titus 2:14 and 1Peter 2:9). A peculiar people cannot expect a democratic nation to pass laws requiring that everyone behave by the peculiar people's own moral standards. Fortunately, this peculiar people has the Holy Spirit of God within them, and when they bring the offer of redemption through Jesus Christ to other people, some of those other people will accept that offer. The Holy Spirit will then come into their lives as well, and those sinners will then want to lead moral lives in order to please God. To attempt holiness any other way is to deny Christ.

8

The Civil Rights of Christians

"Remind them to be subject to rulers, to authorities, to be obedient, to be ready for every good deed" (Titus 3:1)

A CHRISTIAN'S PRIMARY INSTRUCTION with respect to the laws of worldly government is to obey. Romans 13 and other verses state this clearly saying "Let every person be in subject to the governing authorities." There is no reported case in which Jesus violated the laws of the Roman government. While it must have hurt His popularity, He encouraged Jews to pay taxes to Rome. I am writing here only of the secular laws. Jesus, who was Lord of the Sabbath, worked on the Sabbath, and Christians are free from that and other Mosaic laws.

There is, however, a biblical precedent for violating the commands of secular rulers. In Acts 5, Peter was told by the Sanhedrin to cease preaching, and he continued to preach anyway. Since the secular Roman government had granted Jews authority over some matters which would include preaching, Peter's continuing to preach was civil disobedience. It is the only act of civil disobedience by a Christian which is described in any part of the Bible. It is, however, an example to be followed. As Peter said to the Sanhedrin (Acts 5:29) "We must obey God rather than men." The implication is that we are called to only violate the laws of secular government when they are a direct contradiction of the Laws of God.

Many nations of the world have laws which Christians cannot obey without violating their conscience, and in those nations civil disobedience is necessary. China requires pregnant women to have abortions if they already have one or more children. In Israel and in most of the Islamic world, Christians are not permitted to witness to anyone whose parents were not Christians. Some parts of Russia have laws which make it illegal to lead people to a faith which is different than the religion of their ancestors, thereby prohibiting born-again Christians from witnessing to members of the Russian Orthodox Church and other denominations. In all of these cases, we must obey the laws of God rather than the laws of man. This book is written primarily for Christians in the United States and other developed Western nations, and fortunately, we have no laws of this type.

As Christians, we are called to pray, evangelize, assemble, and to take part in the Lord's Supper. We are also called to not violate God's Commandments. If the laws of secular government contradict the Laws of God, then we must choose the Laws of God. Following Paul's example, Christians in the United States should sue to have secular laws rescinded when they violate the laws of God, and Christians have successfully used the courts in the United States for this purpose on many occasions. Recently, in 1998, a Christian landlord whose conscience was violated by local laws which forced him to rent apartments to unwed couples, successfully sued in Federal court to have those laws struck down. Other court rulings have preserved the rights of Christians to evangelize and pray under a wide variety of circumstances. Fortunately, there are few, if any, cases in America and Western Europe in which the laws of man would require us to violate the Laws of God.

Christians are called to pray, and we often hear that prayer in public schools in the United States is prohibited. That is simply untrue. Prayer has always been permitted in public schools in the U.S. In the case of *Widmar v. Vincent* 1981 the US Supreme Court ruled 8–1 that the free exercise of religion permitted students to use the facilities of a public school for prayer and Bible study as long as it was not disruptive to other students. The many Christians who state that prayer is prohibited in public schools in the US are apparently ignorant of the law. Millions of children pray silently in study periods, between classes, and at other times every day in the public schools. It is not illegal, and there would be no effective way to detect this even if it were illegal. Children in public schools also meet both before and after school in classrooms for spoken group prayers arranged by voluntary student clubs. There are no federal laws prohibiting this and, in fact, the Supreme Court has guaranteed this right to students even if the local school authorities try to prohibit it.

The prayer which is prohibited in public schools is public common prayer. The prohibited prayers include prayers which are said aloud in classrooms for the entire class to hear as well as periods of silence in which students are encouraged to pray. Periods of silence in which there is no encouragement to pray are simply study periods and those are held regularly in most schools with many students legally praying.

The only federal court decisions against voluntary student prayer when classes are not in session of which I am aware, are decisions which state that a school is not required to provide faculty advisors for religious clubs in public schools. Since some school districts require that a faculty member be present at all student activities on school property (a rule which I do not find unreasonable), this means that, where no faculty member volunteers to be available without cost to the school district, the students are unable to meet on school property for prayer.

The federal court decisions against student prayer which have received great publicity have been decisions against group prayer and silent periods of meditation during regularly scheduled class time. Those decisions have been in the best interest of Christians since Christians should not want group prayer of an entire public school classroom during regularly scheduled class periods. Classrooms in the United States are likely to have Jews, Muslims, Buddhists, Hindus, atheists, agnostics, and a wide variety of students whose churches use the New Testament of the Bible, but which disagree on fundamental aspects of Christianity. I do not think that I could in good conscience lead a group prayer in such a classroom. It could not be a prayer of worship since I would not want to participate in the worship of a pagan deity. Even if we prayed for some commonly agreed cause, such as our general safety, I do not know how I could word such a prayer. I would normally ask for things from our Holy Father in the name of his only Begotten Son, Jesus Christ. To word the prayer differently in order to not offend believers in a pagan deity would violate my relationship with Christ. To not word the prayer differently would be to expect unbelievers to participate in an appearance of prayer which they believed in their own hearts to be a mockery. This would be offensive to man and God. The alternative of asking the unbelievers not to participate in the prayer which was spoken aloud by the rest of the group would be so offensive to those unbelievers as to make their eventual salvation potentially more difficult. Many Jews and other non-Christians still bear resentment over the way school prayers were conducted prior to the 1962 and 1963 decisions of the Supreme Court prohibiting organized prayers during class time.

Christianity and Politics

I act as the faculty advisor for a club of Christian students who study the Bible and pray together. Our state-supported university provides otherwise unused classrooms for our meetings. The university also offers us a share of the student activity budget, which we refuse each year. There is no reason to refuse our share of the budget except that it might otherwise lead unbelievers to think that we have exploited them financially. Students freely witness to other students. Except when someone solicits my advice or testimony, and for my stating to my students at the beginning of each semester that I am a Christian, my witnessing on campus is limited to other tenured full professors. I really cannot think of any additional privileges which I would want the university to provide to our group or to other student groups.

By comparison to the hardships which Christians have endured throughout history, Christians in the U.S. have a wealth of privileges. Federal courts in the U.S. have consistently upheld the right of Christians to witness. We are generally free to speak in public and to knock on residential doors. We can print and distribute literature. We can evangelize through private radio and television stations. We are virtually unrestricted in our right to assemble on private property.

The restrictions which have been placed on Christians generally concern the use of public property for ceremonial purposes. While we may place nativity scenes on any private property (with the owner's permission), courts have ruled that nativity scenes may not be placed on public property, such as the front of civic centers. It is not clear to me why a Christian would want to place a nativity scene in front of a city hall, when private property is available for that purpose. It is not only an uncompensated transfer of property rights from unbelievers to the Christians seeking to place the nativity scene, but it is one which by its nature is likely to hinder the salvation of unbelievers.

When federal courts recently ruled that cities may not place Christmas trees in front of public buildings, some Christians complained that this infringes on our historical rights to celebrate Christmas. The complaint is confusing. It would be difficult to avoid looking at Christmas trees in any commercial area of the United States during the month of December in 1998, yet Christmas trees were rare in the U.S. before the 1840's. Like Santa Claus, their popularity is mostly attributable to the interests of merchants. Our Puritan forefathers strictly prohibited any celebration of Christmas, noting the pagan origins of most of the customs. They regarded celebration of Christmas as the sin of the Pharisees and scribes in Mk 7:8 where Jesus states, "Neglecting the commandments of God you hold to the tradition of men." Consequently, the long-term historical tradition in America is one of punishing anyone who made even a private display of a Christmas tree. As a Christian, I am happy that public policy is not at either extreme.

9

The Christian's Wealth

"... the grass withers, and the flower falls off, but the Word of the Lord endures forever" (1 Peter1:24–25)

THE PAST FEW CHAPTERS have the apparent implication that it is costly to be a Christian. While everyone else is using politics to have wealth transferred to them, we Christians should not do so. Even defending ourselves on non-Christian issues in this arena may violate our Christian ethics and make us appear worldly and self-seeking. While avoiding political participation is costly, it is only so in a narrow worldly sense. In fact, what is commonly regarded as wealth is only information which indicates that your genes are more likely to survive into the future. Unfortunately, for those with worldly riches, all of this information is based on faith in a system which fails. Because of this, wealth beyond what is necessary to provide the minimum essentials of life is only an illusion. In a prosperous nation such as the U.S., the differences in wealth between different families are themselves an illusion. It is only within this illusion that our pursuit of Christian goals is costly.

The statement that wealth is an illusion must seem odd to come from an economist, but a systematic analysis of wealth shows the truth of this statement. There are different ways of viewing wealth. I have already discussed the fact that property is really only a bundle of rights. While we may think of a material object (land, automobile, etc.) as one's property, all the owner really has is a collection of specific rights which are defined by courts and enforced by the legal system.

Another way economists view wealth is present value. We simply calculate the value of all the likely future benefits which are received by the owner of property, with the values of each of those benefits reduced in value to adjust for the fact that it will be received in the future rather than in the present. This is present value, and it can be applied to value any type of property.

Economists also value wealth based on information. There is general agreement among financial economists that the prices of securities change only with new information. The new information may be related to an economic factor (such as the interest rate), which has effects on the values of virtually all assets, or it can be information which is specific to one company or even to one security which has been issued by a company. Nothing has to change other than information in order for the value of the security to change. For example, if the chairman of the Federal Reserve is heard making a statement which indicates that the Federal Reserve will purchase fewer bonds in the near future, this will affect bond and stock prices as soon as information on the chairman's statement is available. This is true regardless of whether or not the Federal Reserve actually behaves as indicated. As time passes, more information will become available regarding the Federal Reserve's policies on purchasing bonds, and that new information may confirm or contradict the inferences which were made from the chairman's original statement. With each increment of new information, securities' prices will change. In a smoothly functioning market, information is the sole source of changes in the relative prices of securities. Current buying and selling only affects securities prices due to the fact that the current orders to buy or sell are, in themselves, sources of information. If it is generally known that there is a large volume of current orders to buy or sell which do not represent new information in the hands of the parties which placed those orders, or a permanent change in the demand for securities, there will be little to no effect on the prices of the securities traded on those orders.

Information has the same relationship with the values of every other component of wealth. Do you own a piece of land? Actually you own a bundle of rights related to that land, and the market values for each of those rights depends on information. What you can or cannot do with the land depends on the components of the bundle. You may think that you own mineral rights to the land, although those mineral rights can be disputed. Perhaps someone who owns land a short distance from your property discovers oil underneath his property. Immediately, the value of your land will rise, since the existence of oil in close proximity to your land is information which increases the likelihood that your own land has oil. As time passes, you discover more information related to the oil under your land. Perhaps you drill to test for the oil. Your neighbor's oil was only 500 feet below the surface, but the first day you drilled down 500 feet you found nothing. This information means that the probability that you have oil is not as high as you thought, and consequently the value of your land is lower. If you tried to sell the land after that first day's drilling you could not get the price you could have received beforehand. This is true even if you do not disclose the results of the drilling, since any savvy buyer would assume that the reason you are selling is that you have information about the lack of oil.

As you continue to drill, you eventually find oil. The geologist's report indicates that you have a few million barrels and based on current prices of oil and the estimated costs of extraction, you are now (by the standards of the world) a wealthy person. But, nothing has changed except information. You own exactly what you owned before the first neighbor had found oil. Due to new information, you are now rich. Of course, new information on energy prices, costs of extraction, environmental rules, mineral rights of neighbors, etc. could make your oil rights worthless. Seeking to avoid those risks, you may cash in on your newfound wealth by selling your land to an oil company.

By selling the oil rights you receive money, but the value of money is only due to faith in a system. In fact, throughout world history, most monetary systems have not lasted more than a generation. In the history of the world, probably the longest lived system of money with a relatively stable value was the private banking system in Britain where from 1821–1913 pound notes were convertible into gold at a fixed rate. The current monetary system in the U.S. (in which the convertibility of money into gold or any other asset is not guaranteed) has only been around since 1971, and the U.S. price level approximately tripled (money lost two-thirds of its value) in the ten years following the introduction of the new system. Enormous transfers of wealth took place when the U.S. changed monetary systems. Unless you are willing to trust that the monetary system will not experience one of its periodic failures, you will want to quickly convert your money into something else by spending it.

How should you spend your money? Your first reaction may be to enjoy the wealth. You try pure sensual pleasure. You buy expensive foods and silk clothes, but while the anticipation of owning these items may give you a feeling of delight, you soon realize that the actual sensations they produce are meaningless. The next step is to buy expensive material items. Maybe an elegantly furnished mansion with rare art. But what can these do for you? There is no sensual pleasure associated with these items. You can only sleep in one bed at a time. The sensation of a well-made Van Gogh copy is identical to that of an original to everyone except a museum curator.

The pleasure derived from these purchases is psychological. It is the anticipation of impressing other people. From the view point of the materialist philosophers, you enjoy these items because they enhance your likelihood of survival. You can get other people to want to be with you. They will be less likely to oppress you. You will appear more attractive for breeding, and your genes will survive through children and grandchildren. This is the selfish materialistic goal of your wealth.

This pleasure is short lived, however, because the wealthy person never receives the security which is sought. While material objects may bring the association of other people, the relationships are shallow. The wealthy person will never trust other people, knowing that their association was encouraged by material possessions. There is never real closeness and love, only a continual seeking, with hope followed by disappointment. In fact, the people who are attracted to your wealth are the ones whom you can trust least and who will give you the least security and love. You know that if your wealth ever disappears, their association will disappear with it.

After failing to realize any satisfaction or any real improvement in the chances of you genes surviving from conspicuous consumption of your wealth, you give up on the outside world. Instead, you choose to use your money to provide for your family. This is a more direct pursuit of your real goal of gene survival anyway, and the affections of family members can be trusted more than those of strangers. You therefore visit an attorney who draws up a will. After the will is signed, you return home with the assurance that your children have been provided with financial means for their futures.

Have you really provided for their future? Wills are often not carried out as planned by their creators. In the class which I teach for attorneys and accountants on Estate and Gift Taxation, I tell my students that there are a number of conditions, all of which must be simultaneously met in order for a will to be carried out as intended. Someone with an incentive to enforce the will must be aware of its contents. That person must have the mental and financial abilities necessary to seek enforcement, and must be willing to do this in a timely manner. These, and the cooperation of the legal system, are a few of the conditions which are logically necessary to carry out a will, and there is nothing that you can do about this after you are dead. The death of U.S. President Franklin Delano Roosevelt is a good example. The moment before he died he was the most powerful person in the world. The moment Roosevelt died, however, he lost all of his power, and in the days following his death some of the instructions in his will were entirely ignored.[1] He had been naïve to assume that living people would do what a dead person had put in writing, if they did not want to do so, even when that dead person had been the President of the United States.

Let's say that you try to get around these problems by putting the money into a trust to be invested in a diversified portfolio with income to be distributed annually to your children and their descendants. Of course, you must still simultaneously trust the trustee (to carry out the trust instructions), the financial system (so that the assets do not disappear), the economic system (so that the income from the trust still has some purchasing power) and the legal system (so that the trust arrangement and investments have any meaning), but let's ignore those problems for now. As monumental as they may be, they are small relative to the fact that you are trusting your children.

Worldly philosophy tells us that the survival of oneself is the basis for all actions in the world. It is the basis of Darwin. A worldly person who leaves wealth to his children is seeking to help the survival of his own genes. There is the implicit assumption that greater worldly wealth will enable one's children to survive and have children of their own. This will then help the grandchildren and subsequent generations to propagate. While this is an interesting theory, I do not believe that it works in practice, at least in economically advanced countries such as the United States. The theory has implicit assumptions about the behavior of children who inherit wealth, and those assumptions are not borne out by the facts.

Economists looking at the happiness which people express in polls note that there is a correlation between happiness and recent increases in wealth, but none between happiness and wealth itself. Over the twelve years in which I taught at elite private universities, I came to know several students from very wealthy families. I believe that none of them were happier than they would have been if their families were only middle class, and

---

1. Jessica Mitford, *The American Way of Death* (New York: Simon and Schuster, 1978).

The Christian's Wealth

most of them were simply unhappy. This anecdotal evidence is confirmed by the statistic that suicide rates are much higher among the children of the wealthy than among the children of the working class. I also observe that children of the wealthy are more likely to develop drug dependencies and to engage in sexual immorality. This behavior may be at least partially attributed to feelings of personal worthlessness from being unable to support themselves through their own efforts, the fact that many of their friendships appear to depend on their inherited wealth, and the obsession with wealth (rather than family relationships) which they observe in their parents. My readings in the legal histories of wealthy families indicate a very strong relationship between the amounts of inherited wealth and the likelihood of family members to sue each other. Whatever the causes, however, the wealthy are not particularly happy.

Census statistics also indicate wealthy families have significantly fewer children than other families. In fact, the wealthy in the U.S. are less than half as likely to have a large family as any other income group.

There are notable exceptions to the tendency of the wealthy to have small families. Some wealthy people are conscious of the Darwinian goal of proliferation, and purposely have large families and encourage their descendants to do the same. The descendants of Joseph Kennedy of Massachusetts may be an example of this. Can this strategy work? The answer is still no.

First of all, we must remember the observation in the chapter "The Nature of Politics" that every gene which you carry is probably carried by millions of other people. Socially destructive behavior causes a permanent reduction in the food supply of an advanced economy (relative to what otherwise would be produced). Because of this, selfish behavior will reduce the likelihood of the actor's genes surviving. Second, children who are not trained to follow Christ will almost certainly develop personal problems which will interfere with their being able to continue their family's proliferation. When these problems develop even the family's material wealth disappears quickly.

The long-run outcomes for children who are trained to follow Christ are demonstrated anecdotally by the descendants of Jonathan Edwards. Edwards was a Christian preacher in New England in the middle 1700's whose sermons brought spiritual revival to many Americans. He read the Bible and prayed with his children on a daily basis. He was fired by his own congregation (by a vote of 200 to 23) for insisting that only saved Christians could participate in the Lord's Supper, and he subsequently became a missionary to the Indians. He continued to write inspirational sermons which had some readership among Christians. Through the efforts of these Christians, Edwards was appointed president of Princeton University, but he died at the age of 54, shortly after receiving the appointment, and left little in material possessions. By simplistic material standards, his life was a failure.

Was Edwards really a failure? The genealogy of Jonathan Edwards shows him to have had at least 929 descendants. They included 430 ministers of the gospel, 13 university presidents, 86 university professors, 5 U.S. Congressmen and 2 U.S. Senators. That means that by Darwinian standards he was a great success. Even more important, however, he left a spiritual legacy. Edwards helped people better understand Scriptures and he led many souls (particularly Indians) to Christ. Through that, he has an immortal genealogy.

Is this case representative? Based on the Bible and my personal observations, I believe that it is. Children who are trained by Godly parents are protected by the Lord. By contrast, the few available long-term social statistics indicate that most material wealth is relatively short-lived. It is extremely rare for any part of even the largest fortunes to be preserved for more than five generations, and about 90% of large fortunes are entirely dissipated within three generations.[2] While five generations may seem like a long time, it is almost certainly inadequate for any purposes of a selfish believer in Darwin.

I sometimes provide financial advice to wealthy people, and I have found that virtually all of them complain about the fact that their wealth is not enough to make them feel as though they are wealthy. I have heard this in various versions from people with net worths of one million dollars, ten million dollars, and a hundred million dollars. In each case, the person had some disappointment that his wealth did not make him feel wealthy, and in each case the person thought that this problem would be solved by becoming even wealthier than he already was. I believe that this problem comes from an illusion which is held by most worldly people. It is the illusion that if they had a lot of money they would be happy. This illusion is fostered in our culture with movies and advertisements. It makes people seek wealth as their hope of satisfaction and joy. Sometimes people have great excitement when they first acquire a large sum of money, although often this excitement immediately precedes the culmination of a big business venture and

---

2. *The Wall Street Journal* "Lost Inheritance" March 7, 2013.

only lasts for some hours. After the person actually has money in his bank account the reality of how unimportant this money is soon sets in. I can remember the emptiness I felt when, as a non-believer, I sold my first real estate investment at a profit. I was excited about the profit until the day the transaction closed and a deposit was sent to my bank account. I did not feel any better than I had felt before my new wealth, and this fact in itself was a disappointment.

Unfortunately, the typical response is that the wealthy person believes that he is simply not wealthy enough. Based on my experiences, I believe that no one has enough wealth to "feel wealthy" since that feeling will not come from material wealth. The only people who ever tell me that they feel wealthy are born-again Christians who feel great riches from God's love. These people have the satisfaction which others seek from material possessions, and that satisfaction may endure for eternity.

The illusion that material wealth can bring happiness is a great danger. When material wealth becomes our idol, it replaces God in our lives and leads us to sin. Most people want the love of others, and when they see other people pursuing material wealth, they come to conclusion that material wealth would give them the love of others. This leads them to crime and other socially destructive activities in their pursuit of wealth. As Paul states, "the love of money is a root of all sorts of evil" (I Tim 6:10).

The emptiness of wealth also explains why material objects of the highest quality (flawless diamonds, Van Gogh paintings, etc.) sell for such high prices. The owners of large amounts of material wealth have the expectation that they can get satisfaction from material goods. They know, however, that they cannot get satisfaction from what they already own. Hence, the item which is just at the limit of their reach appears to be the item which will give them satisfaction, so they are willing to pay as much as possible for the one item. The disappointment when they acquire that item must be incredible. They are seeking "the pearl of great price" from Jesus' parables, but the only pearls of great price which are worth their cost are in the kingdom of heaven. Those pearls are available to each believer who is willing to pay whatever price is necessary, regardless of how poor or sinful that person may be!

For some people their career becomes the pearl of great price. That is part of why the suicide rate is so high for very successful movie stars, writers, etc. They have sacrificed everything for their success. When that success is obtained, they discover that it was worthless. Since they already have the success which they thought would give them satisfaction in life, there is no place to go. They feel as Mick Jagger did when, at the peak of his career, he sang that he could get no satisfaction. Without salvation and commitment of one's life to Christ, there is no satisfaction.

The illusions from material wealth can be contrasted with the realities of Christianity. People seek love and friendships with their material possessions, but they do not find it. The emptiness of wealth is a stark contrast to the great joy and satisfaction which come from knowing and serving God.

Years ago, before I was saved, one of my students from a very wealthy family told me that his brother had left their mansion in Beverly Hills to become a homesteader in Alaska, where he built his own cabin and lived in it with his wife. I thought at the time that it must be easier to live in a rustic cabin in Alaska knowing all along that you have wealth and a mansion waiting for you when you return. That, however, is the situation of every Christian. Our humble existence on this earth is made easier by the assurance that God has a prepared a heavenly mansion for us. We are his Sons, and our time on earth is only a temporary excursion.

Understanding the futility of wealth helps us to understand why conspicuous display of material wealth is sin. Wealth cannot give satisfaction, but the conspicuous display of material wealth leads other people to believe that it has satisfied us. They become envious of our wealth, and they may steal, deceive, or commit other sins in their attempts to obtain wealth. Both the wealthy and the envious are losers from this process. As James says (James 4:1), "What causes fights and quarrels among you? Don't they come from your desires that battle within you? You want something but don't get it. You kill and covet, but you cannot have what you want." What we want is satisfaction that comes only from mutual love of God and our fellow men. We cannot have that except through Jesus Christ. If we make other people envious, it should only be through what Jesus Christ has done in our lives.

Every deliberate human action is based on faith in a system to produce a desirable outcome. That faith is the motivator of the action. Mistaken faith in the system of this world is Satan's method for making unbelievers into his slaves. Like the unbelievers, Christians base their behavior on faith in information about a system, but our information is the Word of the Lord, and His system does not fail. Those who serve the Lord receive great love from other Christians and an increase in their loving relationship with God. This love is real, and it brings real satisfaction. Unlike material wealth, the benefits of Christianity can last through eternity. Furthermore, the properly instructed children from a Christian family are more likely to be saved through knowing the love of Jesus Christ. They will also have better success and happiness throughout their lives than whatever is achieved by wealthy non-believers. As we are told, we must first seek the things of the Kingdom of Heaven and the things of this world will follow. John 6:29 "Jesus answered, "The work of God is this: to believe in the one He has sent." If we have faith, then we must act in faith. That is why James tells us that faith without good works is meaningless. Our actions are all based on a system of beliefs, and if that system is Christianity, then our faith will give good works. If we do not believe in the one God has sent, then our faith is in the system of this world and it will only lead to desolation.

It is apparent that life is a dynamic process which encompasses the people who live after us, not a static one which ends with ourselves. Hence, wealth is only a link to another end. Every human act is based on faith in the outcome. Therefore all humans live by faith, and it is only a question of faith in the world or faith in God.

10

Israel and Foreign Policy

"In those days the house of Judah will walk with the house of Israel, and they will come together from the land of the north to the land that I gave your fathers as an inheritance." (Jer 3:18)

BECAUSE ISRAEL PLAYS AN important role in Christian prophecy, the U.S. policies with regard to the State of Israel have been a subject of concern and involvement by many Christian groups. It is the most evident part of Christian foreign policy. Due to America's great size and its geographic isolation, American foreign policy is an enigma. The U.S. has more influence on world affairs than any other nation. In fact, in the 1990s, the U.S. is the only remaining great power. At the same time, our size and isolation mean that foreign policy is of less importance to Americans than to the people of any other nation, and, consequently Americans spend less time studying the subject than do the citizens of other developed nations. Americans are left having greater impact on foreign policy than the citizens of any other country while understanding the subject less than the citizens of any other developed country.

For many Americans, our foreign policy with respect to the State of Israel (that is the official name for the nation-state) is inseparable from our treatment of Jews. The persecution of Jews is one of the most disgraceful parts of Christian history, especially since some of this persecution was encouraged by churches. Crusaders were generally permitted to rob any Jews they found. Even Martin Luther, the founder of Protestantism, was so anti-Semitic that he stated Jews should be deprived of "all their cash and jewels and silver and gold" and "that their synagogues or schools be set on

Israel and Foreign Policy

fire, that their houses be broken up and destroyed . . . and they be put under a roof or stable like the gypsies . . . in misery and captivity."[1] Modern clergy have repeated this message. While Christians have attempted to justify anti-Semitic persecution with Mt .27:22–25 in which the Jewish mob urged Pilate to order Christ's execution, the most likely impetuses for persecution are jealousy and ethnic rivalry. Persecution of Jews by persons calling themselves Christians has diminished in the U.S. within my lifetime, but it is still widely practiced in other countries.

Part of the reason for the diminished persecution of Jews in contemporary United States is that many born-again Christians have come to realize that both the Old and New Testaments of the Bible are true, and that the persecution of Jews can only bring God's wrath upon their persecutors. God may choose to punish the Jews for rejecting Him, but the human agents who have attended to this task, from Assyrians and Babylonians to Nazi's have always been punished for their role.

The position of the Christian towards Jews is a delicate one. We know that their religion has failed, and that unconverted Jews are unable to understand the real meaning of their own Scriptures. They are lost, and we have taken their former role by becoming the adopted children of our common God. Yet we know that all of God's promises will be fulfilled and that it is the will of the Lord that all should be saved. Of course, exactly how any of God's promises may apply to Jews is a matter of scriptural interpretation and speculation. In our dealings with Jews our every act should be guided by whether it leads the unsaved closer to knowing Jesus as the Christ through whom they may receive forgiveness of sins. The greatest harm from Christian prejudice against Jews is that it has closed the hearts of Jews to Christianity, thereby preventing them from receiving Christ as their Savior.

Jesus Christ has given us the command to treat all people with love, and that is the best way that we can witness our faith. While the children of Israel play an important role in the Second Coming (Rev 2:14, 7:4 and 21:12), it is not clear that we should have a greater love for unconverted Jews than for other non-believers. Love is an absolute, and God is the Creator, and therefore the Father, of all people, whether they are His obedient children or not. It is also not clear who qualifies as a child of Israel.

There are at least three possible definitions of who is a child of Israel:

---

1. William Shirer, *The Rise and Fall of the Third Reich*, 236.

Christianity and Politics

1. One definition is that the children of Israel are all those who profess the Jewish faith, regardless of their ancestry. The State of Israel has, at times, used this definition to determine who is a Jew. This definition does not make much sense from a Christian viewpoint, however. Christians know that the Jewish faith has been one of not knowing God for over 1900 years. I do not see how profession of that faith, with its consequent rejection of Jesus Christ, could make a person much more important to God. It also makes no sense in terms of applying the Bible to determine the rightful inheritors of land in the Middle East. I find it impossible to believe that the act of rejecting God's only begotten Son qualifies someone for a special inheritance.

2. Some Christians believe that the references to Israel in the later books of the New Testament such as Revelations are really to Christians, since we are now God's children. This view is consistent with Jesus' statement that God could raise descendants of Abraham from stones (Mt 3:9). This also follows from Romans 9:6–9. "For they are not all Israel who are descended from Israel, neither are they all children who are Abraham's descendants, but through Isaac your descendants will be named, That is, it is not the children of the flesh who are the children of God, but the children of the promise are regarded as descendants." This message is repeated in Galatians 3 and it may be inferred from other verses as well. It is certainly a plausible interpretation of the Bible that "Children of Israel" refers to all who believe in Jesus as their Savior, regardless of their biological genealogy.

3. The simplest interpretation of "children of Israel" is that it indicates all of the biological descendants of Jacob, whose name was changed to Israel (Gen 32:28). This implies that the explanation of the "children of Israel" in Romans and the similar verses of Galatians has only a limited application. This is also plausible.

If the phrase "children of Israel" in the book of Revelations only uses the second definition of that phrase, then Jews do not have any particularly important role in the Second Coming, and there is no particular importance to the state of Israel. Since the first definition is clearly irrelevant to the Christian viewpoint, we are left with the third definition as the only relevant one which may give particular importance to the Jewish people (as opposed to other non-believers). Their particular importance to the Christian viewpoint therefore depends on the third definition of "children of Israel" meaning the biological descendants of Jacob. With that in mind, we should look closely at this genealogy. While Paul tells us in 1 Tim 1:4 not to "pay attention to myths and endless genealogies, which give rise to mere speculation rather than furthering the administration of God which is by faith" and that advice is repeated in Titus 3:9, the advocates of special political policies to Israel base their arguments on genealogy, so we should at least test those arguments for internal consistency.

When we try to apply the biblical phrase "children of Israel" to modern situations, it is important that we keep in mind the identity of modern Jews. My experience is that most Christians are unaware that all ethnic Jews descend from the three tribes of Judah, Levi, and Benjamin. The name "Jew" comes from "Jude." These are the people who descended from the tribes of Judea, after Solomon's kingdom of Israel was divided into Judea and Israel. The nine other tribes were taken captive in Assyria around 722 BC. As stated in 2 Kings 18:11 "the King of Assyria deported Israel to Assyria and settled them in Halah, in Gozan on the Habor River, and in the towns of the Medes." These are the so-called "lost tribes of Israel," and evidence indicates that they have been assimilated into the peoples of Syria, Iraq, and the rest of that region. If we use the third definition of "children of Israel," then the survival (and likely assimilation) of the lost tribes is also implied by the book of Revelations. Revelations tells us that the 144,000 will consist of 12,000 from each tribe of Israel. If those are the genetic (as opposed to spiritual) members of each tribe, then each of the lost tribe has survivors to this day. The fact that they are lost tribes, however, means that those survivors do not know that they are descendants of Jacob. They probably consider themselves gentiles, and they and their ancestors have probably married gentiles for the past hundred or so generations.

At least three thousand five hundred years have passed since Jacob's death, and his biological descendants are scattered throughout the world. Despite the numerous possibilities for the loss of ancestral identity, however, there is a scientific basis for believing that many people who claim to be descendants of Israel actually are Jacob's descendants. Jews who have the surname "Cohen" or "Levi" have traditionally been viewed as descendants of Aaron, the ancestor of all Jewish priests. Certain patterns in DNA are passed only from father to son, and since surnames are also passed from father to son, a faithful use of the names "Cohen" and "Levi" would indicate that all persons with those surnames had Levi as their common ancestor. Genetic testing has shown that among persons with the surnames

Christianity and Politics

of "Cohen" or "Levi" that the vast majority have the same distinctive pattern in their DNA, indicating a common male ancestor.[2] While no one can prove that this common male ancestor is Levi, this seems to be the most likely explanation. It does not require too many other assumptions to come to the conclusion that many of the people who consider themselves biological descendants of Israel probably are his descendants.

While many (and possibly the vast majority) of the people who call themselves Jews have Israel as an ancestor, the vast majority of those people have non-Jacobean ancestors as well. Since Jacob lived over thirty five hundred years ago, more than 100 generations have passed since his death. This means that the family tree of every person living today has at least 2 to the 100th power branches in Jacob's generation. Since that figure (approximately 1,267,650,000,000,000,000,000,000,000,000) is about a billion billion times the number of people who have ever lived in the world, there has certainly been intermarriage among Jacob's descendants. It is also evident that there has been some marriage between Jacob's descendants and gentiles. In the first generation, all of Jacob's descendants married spouses who were not descended from him, and this apparently continued for several generations in Egypt. The fact that many Jews throughout the world have skin and hair colorings which are similar to that of the people where those Jews have resided for the past ten or twenty generations indicates that marriage to gentiles has continued. Jews from Northern Europe often have light complexions and sometimes have light hair. Sephardic Jews, from the Middle East, generally have the skin and hair coloring of other Middle Eastern residents. Jews from Africa are mostly black. Based on the differences among Jews in their complexions and hair colorings, my best guess is that for most Jews, many of their ancestors from Jacob's generation were gentiles.

The Old Testament has many descriptions of Israeli's married to Gentiles, with good consequences (like Esther) or bad consequences (like Samson). If the marriages described in the Old Testament of the Bible are indicative of the rate of intermarriage in the population of Israel, then intermarriage was common. King David's own great grandmother, Ruth, was a Moabite, not a descendant of Israel. The men of the tribe of Benjamin married gentile women after (apparently all of) their own women were killed by the other tribes (Judges 20, 21) According to a 1990 report published by United Jewish Communities, the intermarriage rate of Jews in North

---

2. *Wall Street Journal* 5/11/1998.

Israel and Foreign Policy

America is currently over 50 percent.[3] Jews may also be converts with no Israeli ancestry as described in Leviticus 19:34 "The convert should be to you exactly like a born Jew and you shall love him like yourself." Further treatment of converts is described in (Deuteronomy) 10:19, (Exodus) 22:20 and (Exodus) 23:9.

The converse is also true. Many people who identify themselves as gentiles have Israel as an ancestor. The number of Jews grew at a rapid rate in the generations immediately following Jacob so that, while Moses was still living (circa 1250 BC) the male descendants of Israel over the age of 20 numbered 603,550 (Numbers 3:46). The historian Josephus tells us that at the time of the Christ there were about three million people in the world who identified themselves as Jews, and this, of course, excludes the nine tribes which were lost in the Assyrian invasion. The three million Jews constituted about 3 percent of the Roman Empire's population or about 1.5 percent of the world's population. If their proportion of the population had remained constant, and there had been no marriage with gentiles and no loss of faith, then the population of Jews would be about 100 million today. Even adjusting for the Nazi holocaust, this number would be about 90 million. While pogroms against the Jews may have kept the growth of their population below average, this would, at least partially, be offset by the fact that Jews were usually prohibited from participation in the military in the countries and times where those pogroms took place. By contrast, only about 14 million people identify themselves as Jews today.[4]

If we adjust the estimate of 90 million for marriage with gentiles, then the number increases very many times. In the case where two Jews marry gentiles, instead of other Jews, and they have the same number of descendants as a marriage between Jews, the total number of descendants of Jacob through that couple is doubled. This takes place because both the children of the Jewish father and the children of the Jewish mother are descendants of Jacob, by both the general use in English of the term "descendent" and the biblical use of the term "seed." Even if the total population remains constant, the number of descendants for any one person grows geometrically if there is no intermarriage among the descendants. For example, if everyone had only two children who survived to have their own children, the population would remain constant, yet the number of descendants of each person would double each generation. Just as each person living today

---

3. Ibid., 5/20/2002.
4. *The Encyclopedia Britannica* "Book of the Year" 1997.

has more than a billion billion billion upward branches for his family tree in Jacob's generation, each parent in Jacob's generation whose descendants averaged at least two children has at least a billion billion billion downward branches for his family tree. Since there are not that many people in the world, there has certainly been intermarriage.

Estimating an average age at childbirth of twenty-eight years, about seventy generations have passed since the time of Christ when the estimate of the number of Jews was 3 million. If only 3 percent of Jews left the faith of Judaism in each generation, it would be sufficient to explain the fact that the number of Jews grew only to 14 million instead of the 70 million figure which would be proportionate to the growth rate in the rest of the world's population.

After a person converted from Judaism, it would be unlikely for that person's descendants to marry Jews at high rates. For that reason, it would take only a few people converting from Judaism at the time of Christ to produce an enormous number of descendants of Israel who did not identify themselves as Jews. If parents had two children in each generation with no intermarriage among the descendants, then their total descendants after seventy generations would be more than a billion times the world's population. Obviously, that could never take place since marriage partners are limited by the world's population and limited even further by the short geographical distances which most of the world's people have been able to travel. Even when we allow for limited travel, on average, each of the people who at the time of Christ married and had children must have millions of descendants today.

One of the best documented studies of ancestry and descendants shows that the forty-one signers of the Mayflower Compact in 1620 have over 35 million living descendants today. The Pilgrims on the Mayflower were not unusually prolific. This is simply the normal result from the generations over a three-hundred eighty year passage of time without excessive intermarriage. Since converts from Judaism would be unlikely to marry other descendants of Israel, even a few converts from Judaism would produce an enormous number of descendants after 1900 years. We know from the Book of Acts that thousands of Jews converted to Christianity, some living as far from Jerusalem as Rome. So many of the earlier Christians were ethnic Jews, that up through the second century AD, Christianity was generally considered to be a sect of Judaism. With normal fecundity, each of the Jews from the time of Christ who converted to Christianity would

Israel and Foreign Policy

have millions of descendants today, none of whom would be likely to identify themselves as Jews. From this analysis I believe that it is conservative to estimate that there are over one billion people living today as the descendants of the three million people who identified themselves as Jews at the time of Christ, and it is possible that every living person in the year 2000 has at least one Jewish ancestor.

So far, I have only been developing an estimate of the number of descendants of the tribes of Judea. All of the nine tribes of Israel, along with many members of the tribe of Levi, went to Assyria in about 762 BC. According to 2 Kings 17:22 "So the people of Israel were taken from their homeland into exile in Assyria, and they are still there." Anthropological science gives the same conclusion from the genetic marker that has been linked to the tribe of Levi! Researchers in the emerging field of genetic anthropology have visited groups of people in Africa, India, and the Far East who claimed to be lost tribes of Israel. DNA tests on the males of these tribes showed that among some groups, a large number of members had the distinct DNA pattern of the Levi's and Cohen's! Beyond any reasonable doubt, these tribes, which had little intercourse with the rest of the world's Jews for hundreds of years, shared the common ancestor of Levi. Like the Levites, descendants of the nine lost tribes are almost certainly spread throughout the world. Since the Bible indicates that Jews sometimes married gentiles, the best estimate of the number of descendants of the nine Lost Tribes must also be over a billion.

This estimate that Jacob has over a billion descendants living today is not a farfetched mathematical extrapolation. Jacob had 12 descendants (circa 1650 BC), yet four hundred years later the male descendants over the age of 20 numbered 603,550. The population, including women and children probably exceeded two million. This is consistent with the population approximately doubling every twenty-four years. For that population to have reached one billion in AD 2000, the population would only have had to double every 232 years, a very slow rate of growth. As he promised, the Lord is truly making Jacob's descendants "as the sand of the sea which cannot be numbered for multitude" (Gen 32:12).

Where are the hundreds of millions of descendants of Jacob who do not identify themselves as Jews? To some extent they are scattered throughout the world, since some descendants of the Lost Tribes wound up in Asia and Africa. If any American or European family traces its ancestry back several generations, there is some likelihood that they will discover that they are descendants of Jacob. In my own case, my mother's maternal grandmother had the maiden name of Kuhn, a German variation of Cohen. While I have never identified myself as a Jew, it appears from this that I may have had practicing Jews as ancestors only a few generations back

Other descendants of Jacob can be found in virtually every country. Genetic anthropologists have found them as far as southern Africa. To the greatest extent, they are probably concentrated in the Middle East due to the fact that Jacob's descendants lived primarily in Israel but were exiled to Babylon and Assyria. I would expect that the greatest concentrations of unidentified descendants of Jacob would be living close to Jerusalem, since that was the center of Jewish culture for many years.

While many of Jacob's unidentified descendants are probably Christian, my best guess is that most of them are Muslims. The Bible predicted that after the Israelis were carried off into captivity, they would worship other Gods (Dt. 28:64). This is why Israel was carried off into Assyria and, as stated in 2 Kings 17:40, "To this day their children and grandchildren continue to do as their fathers did." Since virtually all of the pagans of the Middle East became Muslims in the sixth and seventh centuries, it is reasonable to assume that these descendants of Jacob converted to Islam. Furthermore, most of the area which has been traditionally inhabited by Jacob's descendants is ruled by Muslims, and the descendants of Jewish and Islamic intermarriage would have had a strong incentive to convert to Islam. Most likely, the descendents of the deported Israelites are living in Islamic countries today with no idea that they have Jewish ancestors. Given that only 14 million people identify themselves as Jews today, and that more than eighty times as many people are Muslim (about 1,125 million in 1997), my best guess is that many more of Jacob's descendants are Muslims than are religious Jews. In fact, not knowing that they were Jewish, the descendants of the nine lost tribes probably intermarried with other residents of the Middle East so it is possible that seventy generations after the Assyrian invasion, most of the world's people who are Muslim have at least one son of Israel as an ancestor (out of their possible one thousand billion billion family tree branches from that generation).

Certainly, many Palestinians have ancestors who were descendants of Jacob. In fact, given the array of genetic possibilities, it is possible that the typical Palestinian whose ancestors had dwelled near Jerusalem for the past nineteen hundred years has as many ancestors who were descendants of Jacob as does a Jew whose ancestors spent most of the past nineteen

Israel and Foreign Policy

hundred years in Europe. Rabbi Dov Stein, Secretary of the New Sanhedrin states about Palestinian Muslims, "There are studies which indicate that 85 percent of this group is of Jewish origin."[5] Many Muslims claim to be descendants of Abraham, and it is probably true that many are his descendants. While few Muslims claim to be descendants of Jacob, it is likely that very many Muslims are also descendants of Jacob.

The significance of the likely Jacobean ancestry of Middle Eastern gentiles is that they would be the owners of most of Israel under Mosaic Law, and it is only under Mosaic Law that the State of Israel can claim ownership of the land. Common law as exercised by British and American courts would clearly leave the property ownership with the Arab Muslims and Christians who held that land prior to 1948. Ezekiel (47:21, 22) states, "So you shall divide this land among yourselves according to the tribes of Israel. And it will come about that you will divide it by lot for an inheritance among yourselves and among the aliens who stay in your midst, who bring forth sons in your midst. And they shall be to you as the native-born among the sons of Israel; they shall be allotted an inheritance with you among the tribes of Israel." Furthermore, we see in Numbers 36:7 "No inheritance in Israel is to pass from tribe to tribe, for every Israelite shall keep the tribal land inherited from his forefathers," and Numbers 36:9 "No inheritance may pass from tribe to tribe for each Israelite tribe is to keep the land it inherits." These instructions are repeated in the book of Ezekiel. That means that the two land-owning tribes of the kingdom of Judah have no biblical basis to the land which was owned by the nine land-owning tribes of the house of Israel.

The Bible also tells us very clearly how much of the land of Israel belonged to each tribe. In Numbers 26:52 " The Lord said to Moses, 'The land is to be allotted to them as an inheritance based on the number of names. . . . 55. What each group inherits will be according to the names for its ancestral tribe.'" The subsequent census is described in Numbers 32, and it shows a total count of 601,730 men. Of those men, 23,000 were Levites who were not permitted to own land leaving 578,730 property-owning descendants of Jacob. Of these, 76,500 belonged to the tribe of Judah and 45,600 were from the tribe of Benjamin totaling 122,100 Jews or .210979 of the population. Hence .78902 of the land belonged to the nine tribes which are not represented among the Jews (the Lost Tribes of Israel).[6] This was subsequently divided into distinct geographical regions for each of the tribes.

5. *God Reports* 12/15/2011.
6. The tribes of Reuben (43,730), Gad (40,500), and Manasseh (52,700) (136,930 total)

Formation of the State of Israel

While the phrase "nation of Israel" is generally used in the Bible to indicate all of the people who are Jacob's descendants, most people today think of the nation of Israel as the secular state which named itself the State of Israel. In order to understand the politics of Israel, it is necessary to have some knowledge about its recent history.

While the anti-Semitism of people in Europe and the United States was the immediate cause for the secular state of Israel, some of the state's roots are in the nineteenth-century Christian millenarian movement. Among others, Sir Laurence Oliphant was "anxious to fulfill the prophecies and bring about the end of the world," and Oliphant brought the Jewish poet Naphtali Herz Imber with him on one of his trips to the Middle East in the late nineteenth century. The works of Imber and subsequent Jewish writers became the impetus for the return of Jews to Zion, often called the Zionist Movement. Christian millenarians may also have had some influence on the strong support which the U.S. showed for the creation of Israel in the 1940s.

Anti-Semitism had existed for centuries in Europe. The old feelings against Jews increased in France in the 1890s as a consequence of the Dreyfus Affair, in which a Jewish diplomat was falsely accused of being a traitor to France. The journalist Theodor Herzl came to believe that while assimilation of the Jews into European society was the most desirable situation, it was impossible to achieve. He therefore began the advocacy of a Jewish homeland in Palestine. Herzl "rejected all narrow nationalism and demanded above all, brotherly consideration for and closest cooperation with, the Palestinian natives in a common homeland." Jewish immigration to Palestine increased, but the hopes of a chartered colony seemed dim due to the anti-Zionist policies of the Turkish government which ruled Palestine.

Britain and Turkey were on opposite sides in World War I, and this offered an opportunity for a political concession to Zionism. The British took Palestine from Turkey during the war. In 1917 the British foreign secretary, Lord Arthur James Balfour gave some support for the Zionist movement

---

received land "on the East side of the Jordan of Jericho toward the sunrise." Hence, the remainder of the land was divided equally among 441,800 property owners with .27637 to the Jews and .72363 to the nine Lost Tribes. The theme of brotherly sharing is continued in Numbers 32 when the Reubenites and Gadites follow the Lord's command by agreeing 32:18 "We will not return to our homes until every Israelite has received his inheritance."

through a letter written to its largest financial supporter, Lord Rothschild. The letter was written partially to gain support of Jews for the British side and possibly also in return for the invention of synthetic acetone by Chaim Weizmann which helped the Allied war effort. Balfour's letter stated "His Majesty's government views with favour the establishment in Palestine of a national home for the Jewish people, and will use their best endeavors to facilitate the achievement of this object, it being clearly understood that nothing shall be done which may prejudice the civil and religious rights to existing non-Jewish communities in Palestine, or the rights and political status enjoyed by Jews in any other country." This statement is the Balfour Declaration which is part of the legal basis for Zionism. Jews asked Balfour to change the words "in Palestine of a national home" to "of Palestine as a national home," but the request was refused. The Balfour Declaration was officially interpreted by the British colonial secretary, Winston Churchill on June 3, 1922 when he wrote that the declaration meant not the "imposition of a Jewish nationality upon the inhabitants of Palestine as a whole, but the further development of the existing Jewish community, with the assistance of Jews of other parts of the world, in order that it may become a centre in which the Jewish people as a whole may take, on grounds of religion and race, an interest and a pride." Until they found out about Britain's secret agreement with France to continue European colonialism in the Middle East, Arabs approved of the Balfour Declaration. King Feisal, who was expected to be the leader of a new Arab state, wrote to the American jurist Felix Frankfurter "We Arabs, especially the educated among us, look with the deepest sympathy on the Zionist movement. We all wish the Jews a most hearty welcome home." The Balfour Declaration was approved by the League of Nations on July 24, 1922.

At the time of the League of Nations' adoption of the Balfour Declaration, the number of Jews in Palestine was 83,790, a little more than 8 percent of Palestine's population, and they owned about 2 percent of the land. Largely as a consequence of persecution in Germany, Jewish immigration to Palestine, both legal and illegal, increased, so that the Jewish population was 445,457 by 1939. That was still only about 30 percent of Palestine's total population, however, with the remainder being made up mostly of Islamic Arabs with some Christian Arabs. It was enough, however, that the Arabs began to fear the loss of their own planned sovereignty. Laws were passed prohibiting the further sale of land to Jews in order to discourage Jewish immigration. When the immigration continued, the Arabs revolted against their British rulers in 1933. The British responded with a "white paper" in

Christianity and Politics

1939 under which Jewish immigration to Palestine was limited to 75,000 people over a 10 year period, and Arabs were assured that the country would not be partitioned or become either an Arab or a Jewish state.

A consequence of the limitation on Jewish immigration to Palestine was that Jews, who were unwanted in Germany and most of Central Europe, had nowhere to go. Hitler wanted to get the Jews out of Germany, but no other nation would take them. In 1938, an international conference convened at Evian, France for the purpose of finding a solution to the problem of Jewish immigration. Leaders of many nations attended, with President Roosevelt representing the U.S. Each nation wanted the Jews to immigrate to a country other than its own however, so the conference ended with no conclusion. In May of 1939 the passenger ship St. Louis arrived at the port of Miami, Florida with 939 Jewish refugees from Germany who sought refuge in the U.S. The U.S. would not permit their entry and, since no other country would take them either, they were sent back to Europe and the holocaust. In part, the refusal of the U.S. to receive large numbers of European Jews in the 1930s was the result of high unemployment of Americans, but it is difficult to imagine that we would have refused the entry of Northern European gentiles who faced similar oppression. As a result of these policies millions of Jews were killed in Nazi gas chambers.

Following World War II the Zionist organization known as the Jewish Agency, demanded immigration visas be issued for 100,000 Jews seeking to immigrate to Palestine. When Britain refused, Jewish terrorist organizations, notably the Stern group and the Haganah, responded with a war against the British. (This war was the principal subject of the book and subsequent movie, *Exodus*.) In July 1946 Menachem Begin's Irgun group blew up a wing of the King David hotel in Jerusalem killing 91 people.[7] During this period Arabs and Jews attacked each other's settlements. In the U.S. Zionists lobbied for the creation of the Jewish state to the extent that President Truman wrote in his memoirs, "I do not think that I ever had as much pressure and propaganda aimed at the White House as I had in this instance." Since 1948 was an election year, Truman was particularly sensitive to losing the Jewish vote. When he issued statements in support of the Jewish refugees in Palestine, Thomas Dewey issued even stronger statements in their support. When one of Truman's advisors presented the Arab view, Truman said that he did not have many Arabs among his constituents. President Truman was also a Southern Baptist who had been exposed

---

7. Truman, 597.

Israel and Foreign Policy

to the millennial teaching that the state of Israel would be created prior to the Second Coming of Christ, so it is possible that Truman was influenced by his own religious beliefs.[8] With the strong support of the United States delegation, the United Nations approved a proposal for the partition of Palestine on November 29, 1947.

On April 9, 1948 Jewish terrorists captured the Arab village of Deir Yasin and massacred virtually all of the (civilian) inhabitants. When news of the massacre circulated throughout the Arab community, about 700,000 Islamic and Christian Arab inhabitants of Palestine fled in fear, leaving only about 155,000 Arabs in the country.[9] By May 13, 1948 the Zionist forces had taken control of all of the territory which the U.N. had allotted to the Jews and part of the territory allotted to the Arabs. The U.N. appointed a mediator on May 14, 1948. This was immediately followed by a message from President Truman to Dr. Chaim Weismann and David Ben Gurion advising them to declare statehood. The State of Israel was declared and immediately recognized, first by the U.S. and then by the Soviet Union. On September 17, 1948 the U.N. mediator was assassinated by Jewish terrorists. A succeeding mediator ordered a truce, but its terms were not observed by either side.

By July 1949, armistice agreements had been made between Israel and its Arab neighbors Egypt, Lebanon, Transjordan, and Syria. Under the agreement no entity remained that was officially called Palestine. When the Palestinian Arabs (both Muslims and Christians) who had fled in terror returned, they found their homes and farms now occupied by Jews who were given new titles to the property. The Palestinians were dispossessed of all of their property and their hopes of a nation. Many of these people had never been involved with any political movements or taken any stand against the Jews. Regardless of any political participation, the Palestinians became refugees and many remain so today. Some have spent their lives in refugee camps and do not hold passports or citizenship from any nation. On December 11, 1948 the U.N. adopted a resolution stating that Israel must allow Palestinians whose property had been confiscated the option of receiving the return of their property or monetary compensation. This proposition has been re-affirmed every year by the U. N., but has never been implemented. In 2002 Israel stated that it will not allow more than 100,000 of the displaced Palestinians to return, that it will not provide

8. Hefley, 1978.
9. Encyclopedia Britannica.

compensation to any of the Palestinians whose property was confiscated, and that it regards this position as non-negotiable.[10] Israel has subsequently passed laws which would provide monetary compensation to Palestinians whose property was confiscated, but those laws have several conditions for receiving that compensation including a difficult procedure for establishing prior ownership, acceptance of the sovereignty of the State of Israel, and renouncing all future claims against Israel. Despite a somewhat extensive search in late 2011, I was unable to find evidence indicating that any payments have been made.

Despite the armistice, Israel's Arab neighbors were unhappy with the situation and sympathetic to the plight of the Palestinian refugees. They staged guerrilla raids against Israel, and Israel responded by joining France and Great Britain in attacking Egypt in 1956. In 1967 another war began with Syria's announcement that Israel was massing troops on its border. Egypt signed mutual defense pacts with Syria and Jordan. Israel then made a pre-emptive strike, destroying most of the Egyptian forces. In 1973 Egyptian forces attacked Israel on Yom Kippur, the holiest day of the year to Jews. In each of these wars, Israel was victorious.

Since 1967 the Palestinian Liberation Organization and other groups of Palestinian refugees have waged a war of terrorism against Israel and its supporters. This terrorism has included the massacre of Israeli athletes at the 1968 Olympics in Munich Germany and hijackings of planes and ships.

Historically, most Jews have not been Zionists. In 1919 many of the leading Jews in the United States published a full page protest against the establishment of a Jewish state in Palestine and asserted that out of 3.5 million Jews in the U.S., only 150,000 were Zionists. Albert Einstein warned in 1938 that the return of a political nation to Jews would hurt their spirituality.[11] Religious Jews have always believed that there would be a return to their homeland led by the Messiah, and most have thought that it would be improper to start a state without Him. The belief that Israel should not have been created until the coming of the Messiah was so strong among the Kartas (a group of Orthodox Jews who have lived in Palestine for hundreds of years) that they say that the Nazi Holocaust was God's punishment for Zionist efforts. The Kartas still refuse to pay taxes to Israel or to handle currency with pictures of Israel's Zionist founders. Even today, the 15 percent of Israeli Jews who are most Orthodox in their beliefs state that Israel

10. CNN On-line 4/12/2002.
11. Hefley 1978.

Israel and Foreign Policy

should not have been created.[12] Nonetheless, polls showed that by 1947, 80 percent of American Jews supported Zionism.

In the U.S. today, support for the secular state of Israel is a principal tenet of many groups of Christians seeking to influence politics. As a result of this support and the influence of American Jews, cutting aid to Israel is referred to as "the ultimate political taboo."[13] As of 1998 United States pays $3 billion per year to Israel in foreign aid and approximately another $3 billion to Egypt which receives matching aid under the Camp David accords. This is in addition to the U.S. guarantee of some Israeli loans which are otherwise of dubious marketability. In order to put this into perspective, the total of all foreign aid given by the U.S. in 1997 was $9.6 billion per year, so Israel and Egypt received 63 percent of America's foreign aid. While Israel and Egypt are not rich nations, they are by no means poor, and unlike much of the third world, the citizens of Israel and Egypt are not starving or dying from easily treated diseases. While the U.S. was generous to the world in the years immediately following World War II, that generosity has diminished greatly, and if we exclude the aid given to Israel and Egypt, the U.S. rate of giving, both private and public, is among the lowest of developed nations. While Americans give significant portions of their income to churches, universities, museums and other public charities, in 1990 the per capita giving by Americans to developing countries was only $47 from public sources (such as the federal government) and another $10 from private charities. By comparison, fifteen Western European nations had an unweighted average of per capita gifts to developing nations of $152 from public sources and $10.50 from private charity (1993 U.S. Statistical Abstract,) These other nations give more than Americans despite the fact that born-again Christians are an insignificant percentage of their populations, and also despite the fact that Americans are wealthier than the citizens in most of those other countries. (The average American still has a higher standard of living than the average citizen of any other country.) Since evangelical Christians constitute about 30 percent of the U.S. population, these statistics indicate that, including each individual's share of public funds, and even if all of the private donations come from evangelical Christians, the average evangelical Christian in the U.S. still gives less money to the poor in developing nations than does the average West European unbeliever. Recent figures on aid given to refugees from

---

12. *Newsweek*, April, 1998.
13. *Wall Street Journal* 6/26/1998, A16.

Christianity and Politics

the war in Kosovo showed that the U.S. had given approximately as much as Canada, but that tiny Switzerland had given more aid than both Canada and the U.S. put together. Even the heathen show more generosity to the poor than do Americans, and our stinginess makes us a bad example.

Some Christians have carried their strong support for Israel to the point of animosity for Muslims. Animosity can never be part of Christian behavior. Ethnic prejudice is equally unChristian, and it is even beneath the standard of unbelievers in developed countries. Nonetheless, while the U.S. has made illegal virtually all manifestations of ethnic and religious prejudice, I often hear ethnic slurs cast at Palestinians and other natives of the Middle East. The university community is generally known for its racial and ethnic tolerance, but I have heard a teacher at a leading university refer to people from the Middle East as "tent-heads" and "camel jockeys." A very reliable source told me that a few years ago a graduate of the school of business at a large Midwestern university offered the school a gift which was so large that it would have been the largest donation in the university's history. The graduate asked only that a building on campus be named after his father. Primarily, due to the fact that the father's name was Arabic, the gift was refused with the reason stated that it would create too much controversy. Based on my personal observations, the prejudice against people from the Middle East in the United States today is comparable to the prejudice against Jews one hundred years ago. Since the Semitic people are all of the people of Middle Eastern origin, prejudice against Arabs is the greatest form of anti-Semitism in the U.S. today. Since Jacob was an ancestor of most people of Middle Eastern origin, animosity toward people from the Middle East is also the greatest prejudice against the descendants of Israel.

Sincere Christians were among the leaders of the movements in the U.S. to eliminate unfair treatment based on race and ethnicity. While I dispute the propriety of some of the methods of those Christians, their participation was part of the Christian mandate against ethnic and racial prejudice. A half century ago, sincere Christians were offended by the unfair treatment of blacks and Jews in the U.S. In a similar way, Christians today should be offended by the unfair prejudice which is openly shown in the U.S. against natives of the Middle East and their descendants.

Our every action in front of non-believers must be judged by the criterion of whether it brings those unbelievers closer to receiving Jesus as their savior. About 20 percent of the world's people are Islamic, and our behavior toward them has made it more difficult for them to open their hearts to Jesus Christ.

Analysis

Christians know that all things go according to God's plan and all things work for the good of those who love the Lord. The assimilation of the nine lost tribes of Israel into the populations of Iran and Iraq was therefore part of God's plan. God states in the Bible that his plan was to divide the land of Israel among the tribes, and that land could not be transferred from tribe to tribe. He did this knowing that the owners of over 70 percent of Israel's land would be taken into Assyria and that their descendants would become Muslims. The Bible also tells us that God's plan includes reconciliation and peace between the houses of Israel and Judah. (Ezekiel Chapters 32–37). After discussing the joining of the house of Israel with the House of Judah (Ezekiel 37:17–20), God says "I will take the Israelites out of the nations where they have gone. I will gather them from all around and bring them back into their own land." This clearly refers to the house of Israel, as opposed to the house of Judah since the previous verses dealt with the joining of Judah and Israel, and the subsequent verse (Ezekiel 37:22) states "I will make them one nation in the land, on the mountains of Israel. There will be one king over all of them and they will never again be two nations or divided into two kingdoms." The chapters which follow these chapters discuss the attack on Israel by Gog, Persia, Cush, and Put, and have a description with similarities to the description of attacks described in the Book of Revelations.

As already noted, the principal impetus for the birth of Israel was the anti-Semitism of Europeans and Americans. The only real explanation for this anti-Semitism is that it was based on racial rather than religious reasons. Its purpose was that another race suffer and die so that the inflicting race had a greater chance of survival. This is exactly what the Nazis attempted with their concentration camps. It is also the reason why the U.S. and the rest of the world refused to receive Germany's Jews when they tried to immigrate. It was purely Darwin and the politics of Satan.

Just as evangelism for Christ is contagious, so is selfish behavior at the expense of others. Jews learned from their mistreatment by gentiles and came to believe that their own survival required that they play the same game. They declared their own state and confiscated the personal property of the Palestinian Arabs. When the Palestinians failed to re-gain their former property through the military efforts of Arab nations, many came to believe that they would only succeed through terrorist actions of their own. It is understandable that they came to this conclusion. They had witnessed

Christianity and Politics

the creation of Israel as the outcome of the terrorist acts of Jewish organizations from 1945–1948. During that period Jewish terrorists massacred civilians, assassinated diplomats, and blew up a hotel. The people who committed these acts of terrorism became Israel's Prime Ministers. They did not hide their terrorist acts, but proclaimed them since these acts were the strongest part of their credentials, just as participation in the American Revolution was the strongest credential of any politician in the early history of the United States. The dispossessed Palestinians believed that they had little to lose and everything to gain by terrorism.

Christians have voted and organized politically so that the United States would give unqualified support for the State of Israel.[14] This has meant supporting the continued confiscation by the house of Judah of the land which belongs to the house of Israel. Most of that land does not belong to the house of Judah by Mosaic Law or by modern common law. Christian political action has created animosity among Muslims for Americans in general and for Christians in particular. It has hardened the hearts of the house of Israel, making it harder for those people to accept Jesus as their Savior.

In defense of the Israelis, almost every new state begins with violent acts against the old government, and it is still common in the Middle East for the state to confiscate the property of whole segments of the population when their leaders have been rebellious. The Romans confiscated the property of Jews without note when they destroyed much of Jerusalem and enslaved its people in 70 AD. Nazis also confiscated the property of Jews. This has not been the general practice in the modern developed world, however, and after World War II Germany was forced to pay reparations to Israel as compensation for lost property and lost lives. The State of Israel confiscated the property of Islamic and Christian Arabs purely based on religion and the fact that it was abandoned when they fled Jewish terrorism.[15] This situation produces a great deal of animosity for Israel throughout the world. Even if the Palestinians are not descendants of Jacob, Israel's treatment of them violates the biblical commands of hospitality to aliens and specifically violates Numbers 15:15 which states "The community is to have the same rules for you and for the alien living among you; this is a lasting ordinance for the generations to come. You and the alien shall be the same before the Lord."

14. see *Wall Street Journal* 5/23/2002.
15. Hefley, 1978.

Israel and Foreign Policy

Observers including Christian missionaries have stated that the Palestine Liberation Organization would have no power if the financial and other injustices against individual Palestinians were repaired.[16] According to the Jerusalem Post May 16, 1948, Israel's GDP for 1948 was estimated at 100 million Israeli pounds which converts to $400 million U.S. dollars. Federal Reserve statistics for the U.S. indicate that the total value of U.S. real estate in 1999 was about $12.4 trillion while US GDP for that year was about $9 trillion. If we assume that the Arabs who left Israel were 40 percent of the population, owned 40 percent of the real property, and that the ratio of real property to GDP in Israel in 1948 was the same as for the US in 1999, then the value of property confiscated in 1948 was about $220 million. At 6 percent interest per year, the value of that amount in 2012 would be $9.17 billion. While this is a crude estimate, it should give us the scale order of the true current value of the property confiscated by Israel. Relative to the prolonged costs of the conflict in the Middle East, $10 billion is a small amount of money. I therefore asked an associate who had contacts with Middle Eastern governments why one of the nations which is concerned with the problem of Palestinian refugees does not simply compensate the Palestinians for their lost property, thereby taking away much of the problem. My associate agreed that the cost of compensating the Palestinians would be an amount which was affordable by the major Arab nations, but he said that none of them would want to compensate the Palestinians. This is due to the fact that the prolonged suffering of the Palestinians strengthens the governments of the Islamic nations.

Extremist groups in many Islamic nations exploit the plight of the Palestinian refugees in a similar way to the Zionists' exploitation of the plight of Jewish refugees after World War II. Television news programs throughout the Islamic world daily show films of Palestinians being beaten by Israeli soldiers and houses of dissidents being blown up. These hate-inspiring displays make the public recognize the need for their own government to stay in power, and they justify large military budgets.

Since Israel's current GDP exceeds $100 billion, why don't the Jews compensate the Palestinians for their lost property in order to eliminate the influence of the PLO? It is the same answer. Extremist political parties benefit from the ongoing conflict. Publicity about the terrorist acts of the PLO brings voters to continue supporting the extremists. The one thing on which the extreme Arab and Jewish groups can agree is that they want the conflict to continue.

16. Ibid.

Christianity and Politics

The philosophers of selfishness at the expense of others are the philosophers of Satan. The people who follow their instructions are the victims of an elaborate trick. They think that they are helping themselves at someone else's expense, but they are usually the ones who are hurt most. The situation in Israel is that of one group of the descendants of Abraham and Jacob trying to help the chance of their own genes surviving by oppressing another group of the descendants of Abraham (and probably Jacob.) The inevitable outcome is that the descendants of Abraham and Jacob are the losers.

The Jews and Palestinians are brothers who worship the same God. All Muslims believe that the God they worship, Allah, is the God of Abraham, the same God who is worshipped by Jews. Most Christian seminaries accept that Muslims worship the same God as do the Jews. I have heard Christians assert that Allah is actually the pagan deity Bael, but the basis for this assertion is weak. Bael was an idol and the Koran specifically denies the divinity of all idols. It is difficult to put much weight on the fact that the pronunciation of Allah is different than the pronunciation of the name of the LORD of Israel, since we do not know that name's pronunciation. Since the name of the LORD was sacred, and Jews feared the name being profaned, it is shown only by the Hebrew letters indicating YHWH. While this is usually pronounced Jehovah or Yahweh, we are not certain of the correct pronunciation of YHWH. Virtually all Christians in Islamic countries use the name Allah in their Bibles and their prayers. If the pronunciation of the name of God as "Jehovah" or "Yahweh" is crucial, then we must state that many of our Christian brethren are not worshipping God since they pray to Allah.

Christians know that the Koran is false in every place that it differs from the Bible, and because of the false teachings of the Koran, Muslims do not know the correct character of God. Christians also know that unconverted Jews do not know the correct nature of God, since they do not know Jesus Christ and the true meaning of Old Testament Scriptures. Even though the Muslims know some of Jesus' teachings and that He will return in the Last Days, they believe that He was only a man and that He did not die on the cross. By comparison, the Jews rely on the Tanach (Torah, Nevi'im, and Kesuvim) which constitutes what Christians call the Old Testament of the Bible. They also follow the Talmud which has interpretations from Rabbi's who lived between 188AD to about 1044 AD. The fact that the Jews know the Old Testament without the confusing influence of the Koran may mean that the Muslims have the greater error in their knowledge of the character of God. Since both are in error, however, I do not know that there

Israel and Foreign Policy

can be much importance to one group having a greater error than the other or even how such a measurement can be made. As stated in Isaiah (8:14) "and he will be a sanctuary, but for both houses of Israel he will be a stone that causes men to stumble and a rock that makes them fall." I believe that this reference to Christ indicates that the house of Judah stumbles under Judaism while the house of Israel stumbles under Islam. From a broad perspective, Islam and Judaism are very similar religions. The Muslims state that they are worshipping the same God as the Jews, and I believe that we should accept that on its face.

As with all other matters, the Christian position on Israel must be based on the Bible and on serving as good witnesses for Jesus Christ. History tells us that if we oppress the children of Israel we will bring God's wrath on ourselves. Literal interpretation of the Bible may (or may not) require that Israel exists as a nation in the end times.

I recently listened to the radio broadcast of a prominent millennial Christian in which he criticized the U.S. government for placing conditions on Israel's behavior prior to the U.S. guaranteeing $10 billion in loans to the State of Israel. (The US guarantee of loans made to the State of Israel is in addition to foreign aid.) The import of his message was that the U.S. should support the government of Israel unconditionally. This unconditional support of the government of Israel is a principal tenet of many political groups made-up of born-again Christians. They believe that this is called for in the Bible, since those who bless the children of Israel will themselves be blessed.

While the Bible states that those who bless the children of Israel will themselves be blessed, blessing the children of Israel does not mean unconditional support for the secular State of Israel. The Bible tells of many kings of Israel who were wicked. Injustice to the poor and the neglect of God were the principal crimes of most of these kings. Israel today has been unjust to its poorest residents. It is a secular nation, not a religious one. Only a minority of its residents attempt to keep the Orthodox laws. Christian missionaries to Israel have told me that atheism is rampant there. Would God have thought worse of the ally of a wicked Israeli king if that ally required changes as a condition for aid? I do not think so.

Some people attempt to justify U.S. aid to Israel through the U.S.'s military needs. The argument is that Israel is the U.S.'s only friend in an economically important area of the world, and therefore we must continue the alliance. The argument is circular due to the fact that our support for Israel is the principal reason that we have lost the friendship of other nations in the Middle East. Prior to 1948, the U.S. had good relations with most of the nations in the Middle East.[17] As already described, Israel is disliked by its Islamic neighbors, due to religious differences and also due to its confiscation of private property previously owned by Muslim citizens. Giving Israel the majority of U.S. foreign aid made us disliked by those neighbors. Egypt quickly switched sides, however, when we gave them equal aid. Probably any nation would agree to be our temporary ally if we paid them billions of dollars per year in aid. It is particularly true in Israel's case because its alliance with the U.S. serves to avert the threat that other large nations (such as Russia and Western European nations) would intervene against it.

I expect that the military argument will be advanced in the coming decade since Israel and the U.S. have tentatively agreed to a gradual elimination of economic aid to both Israel and Egypt with a substitution of increased military aid for Israel alone. Since Israel already has a large military budget, increasing Israel's military aid will enable it to decrease its own spending for military purposes. The net effect is exactly the same as if we continued to give economic aid to Israel, and only the rhetoric will change.

What Christians Should Do

Our Lord has told us that to hate someone is the same as committing murder, and Christians should hate neither Jews nor Muslims. Jesus asks us to be peacemakers and tells us that we will have blessings for this. We are also told to show unselfish charity and to be good witnesses for Christ. The situation in Israel is a great opportunity to do all of these.

First, Christians should stop making vitriolic statements about Muslims. Those statements are often untrue and, either way, they make the goal of leading Muslims to salvation more difficult.

We also need to cease supporting political violence in the Mideast. That means that we must stop our own efforts that bring the US to continue its aggressive policies against Afghanistan and Iraq and closer to war with Iran. We must also stop political support for policies which perpetuate the confiscation of property and other injustices against Palestinians. We need to keep in mind that those Palestinians are mostly the descendants of Jacob, so they are as much the children and nation of Israel as are the Jews.

---

17. Truman, p. 597

Israel and Foreign Policy

We need to bring the good news of salvation through Jesus Christ to the Jews and Muslims living in Israel. While this would be illegal under Israeli law, I have already noted that the one instance of civil disobedience in the book of Acts was when Peter told the Sanhedrin that he would continue to witness for Christ in violation of the orders of the Sanhedrin. Christians should be eager to witness in Israel, even though it violates the laws of the state since, ultimately, peace will only come through the presence of Christ in the people of that region.

I have already noted that the inflation adjusted value of all of the confiscated Palestinian property is probably under $10 billion. This figure is insignificant compared to the costs of war in the Middle East. While Israel does not recognize this as a debt, history tells us that the debt will get paid, since in modern times virtually all developed nations have been compelled to compensate non-citizens for their confiscated property. In compensation for the financial damage of the Holocaust, Germany has paid billions of dollars in reparations to surviving Jews and to the State of Israel. Eastern European nations which have been liberated from Soviet socialism have repatriated property to its former owners. Switzerland is currently in the process of making restitution of Jewish property which was improperly handled by Swiss banks during the Holocaust. Russia has even been compelled to pay the principal on bonds issued by the Czar which were sold to foreign investors. Old claims for property persist, and are the cause of conflict until they are settled.

A quick settlement of Israel's debt to the Palestinians is in everybody's long-run interest. It would stop the descendants of Jacob from killing each other. Fighting between brothers is one of the major continuing themes of the Old Testament. It took place between Cain and Abel, between Isaac and Ishmael, between Esau and Jacob, and between the sons of Israel's kings. While God wills all things, it is not His desire that His children should fight each other. The books of the major prophets of the Old Testament (such as Ezekiel) indicate a return to peace and sharing ownership of land. This is in line with the New Testament under which all men are brothers without regard to race. If Christian acts can help to bring peace between the children of Jacob (Israel), then we may be blessed as peacemakers.

Since 70 million Americans claim to be part of evangelical Christian churches, Israel's $10 billion debt to the Palestinians would only come to about $150 from every evangelical Christian in the U.S. That is about one day's wage for the average American.

Christian payment of Israel's debt to the Palestinians would be analogous to Christian's buying slaves and setting them free prior to the Civil War. It may seem unfair to the Christians, but the issue of unfairness is only a narrow view that misses the whole point. If we have given our lives to Christ, then the only good thing is to serve Him. While Israel has periodically stated that it will not provide compensation to the Palestinians, it will allow Western states and humanitarian organizations to compensate the Palestinians.[18]

While most of the benefits to payment of this debt would be realized by Israel and the Palestinian Arabs, we may have great material benefits for ourselves. Prolonged conflict in Israel is very costly to the U.S. due to both foreign aid and the availability of cheap oil. From these two considerations, the U.S. may save the $10 billion in a short time.

The greatest importance of this is in serving God. It is only from the narrowest of perspectives that the conflict in Israel is one of Jews against Muslims. It is Satan against all of God's people, and God's people include many who are now Jews and Muslims. The Lord wants these people to be saved and the conflict prevents this.

If the conflict in Israel is the prelude to the Armageddon, then it is all the more important that Christians act as good witnesses. The Lord does not need or want us to bring about the horrors of the book of Revelations. If Christians act in a charitable way to both the Jews and Arabs in Israel, then new souls will be led to receive Christ. Hebrews 12:14 tells us "Pursue peace with all men, and the sanctification without which no one will see the Lord," and this is a central message which is repeated throughout the Old and New Testaments. Let us follow Christ's instructions, here and in all other matters.

---

18. CNN On-line 4/12/2002.

11

Preparation for the End Times

"I testify to everyone who hears the words of the prophecy of this book: if anyone adds to them, God will add to him the plagues which are written in this book; and if anyone takes away from the words of the book of this prophecy, God will take away his part from the tree of life and [i]from the holy city, which are written in this book." (Rev 22:18–19)

THE IMMINENCE OF THE Second Coming of Christ is not a political question, but Christian beliefs on this subject have influenced political behavior. Many evangelical Christians believe that we are in the final generation before the Second Coming, and the international political viewpoints of those Christians are dominated by their beliefs concerning the Second Coming. Some evangelical Christians were active supporters of the 1991 Gulf War, at least partially due to beliefs that this war was a battle leading up to the ultimate Armageddon. Evangelical Christians who believe that Christ's Second Coming is imminent influence the U.S.'s treatment of Israel, and numerous other foreign and domestic issues.

Jesus plainly stated that His coming will be as unexpected as that of a thief in the night, so Christians must be prepared at all times for the Second Coming. The prophesied element of surprise in this event implies that no Christian should ever believe that the Second Coming will not be within his own lifetime. Every believer must always live with that possibility. While no Christian can have grounds for saying that the Second Coming is not imminent, the Bible offers prophetic signs of the Second Coming, so it is possible that Christians may believe that the Second Coming is imminent. In this chapter I will address the questions of whether current events are fulfillment of prophecy for the signs of Christ's Second Coming, and, if we have prophetic signs of the Second Coming, should we change our political behavior.

At the close of the twentieth century, many Christians, ranging from born-again fundamentalists to worldly citizens who have only the barest knowledge of the Bible believe that Christ's return is now imminent. Part of the reason for this widespread belief is purely secular. The world is changing at an increasing rate. The changes in technology, social conditions and many other aspects of life in the last two decades of the Twentieth century have been so great that it is difficult to even imagine the end of the next century. It is also satisfying to some people to think of themselves as part of the last generation rather than as just one more link in the many generations of Christians leading up to the Second Coming, and this narcissistic view may be part of the reason why so many Christians today have this interpretation.

Many sociological variables have increased over time at a geometric rate. These include population, per capita incomes, speed of transportation, increase in human knowledge, and the ability to communicate. Population is probably the steadiest and most easily measured of these variables, and the approximate growth has been from 200 million people at the time of Christ, to 500 million in 1650, 1 billion in 1850, 2 billion in 1930, 3 billion in 1960, 4 billion in 1975, 5 billion in 1990 and 6 billion in the year 2000. While it took over a thousand years for the population to double at the beginning of the Christian era, the world's population now doubles in less than 30 years.

Clearly, the change in sociological variables in the twentieth century is rapid by the absolute standard of man's ability to absorb and adjust to new information. When it took a few centuries for the population to double, some sociological variables were predictable over a person's natural life span. Those same variables are not predictable for young people who are living today. The possibilities that pollution might destroy all life, or that computers and robots might replace all production workers were not real possibilities during the lifetimes of the people of the eighteenth century. They are real possibilities for young people today.

One problem associated with the rapid change in modern times is the growth in size of urban areas. Partially due to improved transportation, and partially due to needing fewer people on farms to feed the world, metropolitan areas have been growing at increasing rates. This may be one of the most important sociological changes of the modern era, since large cities

Preparation for the End Times

with mobile populations mean that people can no longer depend on the personal relationships which underlay most human intercourse in previous centuries. In a small community with little mobility, everyone would eventually discover who was honest and reliable, and who was not. Since this was known to everyone in the small community, those who were not honest and reliable were certain to be punished for their behavior. The certain threat of punishment enforced morality. Hence, most people could depend on relationships with other people in their community.

A big city with a mobile population is different in this respect. If someone cheats other people, it is not likely to become known to everyone else in the community. As long as there is no violation of the law, or the law is not enforced, the cheater can profit from his immoral behavior. This means that the enforcement of moral codes which took place in the small immobile community is not present in the large mobile community, and immoral behavior will result. Without enforcement, moral codes disappear. Fortunately for Christians the Holy Spirit is continually enforcing God's morals on us.

Commerce is based entirely on trust. If the person with whom you deal is entirely untrustworthy, there is no guarantee that the untrustworthy person will not simply take your money and give you nothing in return. Because of this possibility, some trust is necessary for any transaction to take place. As personal trust disappears, it becomes necessary to do business in other ways if any transactions are to take place. Technology can provide a substitute for personal trust through electronically verified credit card transactions, but this implies a substitution of technology and trust in financial institutions for trust in personal relationships, and that substitute becomes increasingly necessary in our increasingly mobile society. Since repeated reinforcement of the trust in personal relationships makes those relationships stronger, the substitution of technology for personal relationships can make our hearts grow colder than they would be under the old system.

While these problems portend a certain end to the world as we know it, they are secular in origin. Of course, every event which takes place is part of God's plan, and God has used secular events to fulfill His prophecies throughout history. There are good secular theories for Israel's military success under King David and its subsequent conquest by the Assyrians. Those theories may be correct. They were simply the tools which God used to carry out His plan. Similarly, the secular dangers on the world's horizon at the close of the twentieth century are not by themselves a sign of God's intentions, but God may choose to use them to fulfill prophecy.

Christianity and Politics

Christians should also remember that not all of the secular forces of modern times lead to calamity. Many of these forces are helping mankind. Diseases are being cured at increasing rates. Longevity has also increased at increasing rates, so that for Americans it is currently growing at around 3 years per decade. (Permanent growth in longevity at the rate of 10 years per decade would mean that no one dies.) Per capita incomes are growing throughout the world and, as a rough approximation, they are doubling every 30 years, even after adjusting for inflation. The enforcement of electronic surveillance could produce consistently honest behavior among people. Computerized prosthetic limbs can let the lame walk while other advances may let the blind see. Christians know, however, that the return to Eden cannot take place through the efforts of man. It can only take place through reconciliation with God. While the twenty-first century could be a very nice time to be alive, it could also be so terrible that people will beg for Christ's return.

Christ's return will be the ultimate event of history, and this event has been imminently expected by many Christians in the past. Christians had expected the Second Coming in the First, Second, and Third centuries AD. Large numbers of Christians falsely predicted that Christ would return in 800 AD, 1000 AD and 1033 AD. Thomas Muntzer predicted Christ's return in 1525. There have been many modern predictors of Christ's return beginning with William Miller (1844), Wovoka (1890) and John Chilembwe (1915). Jehovah's Witnesses have made at least three specific predictions of Christ's return in the Twentieth century, and revised their statements after each prediction failed to take place.

Predictions of the Last Days surged with the publication of Hal Lindsey's *The Late Great Planet Earth* in 1970. Over the next few years, some of Lindsey's predictions seemed to be realized. The USSR (viewed by Lindsay as the biblical Gog) increased its military power, and the Middle East became wealthier from high oil prices. Meanwhile, in the US, rates of murder, abortion, and divorce grew. Partially due to this affirmation of prophecy, sales of Lindsey's book increased and more Christians came to believe that the Last Days were imminent.

When we measure whether or not Lindsey's predictions have been realized, the comparisons are best made with conditions at the time that Lindsey's book was already popular. The reason is that many authors write books making predictions, but only the subset whose predictions have some immediate truth become popular. Since only popular books are ever going to influence people and be studied, we need a way of determining if these authors were really able to make predictions with more than a random chance of becoming true. It is analogous to forecasters of the US stock market. There are many forecasters, and it will always be the case that some of them will have a few successful years in a row. Those forecasters will consequently receive a great deal of publicity. This tells us nothing about the forecasters' ability, however, since some of them must be succeeding purely by chance. It is only an indication of a forecaster's ability when the predictions have been so accurate as to make the forecaster popular, and the forecasts continue to be accurate long after the forecaster has become popular.

Lindsey's forecasts failed after he became popular to such an extent that it does not take sophisticated analysis to show that his predictions were inaccurate. In fact, his forecasts show less accuracy than we would expect from random guesses, not only from the time he was popular (about 1980), but even from the time he first wrote *The Late Great Planet Earth* (1970).

The major specific forecasts of Lindsey's final chapter "Polishing the Crystal Ball" are:

1. movement of Christian churches away from the literal truth of the Bible
2. persecution of genuine Christians by mainline denominations
3. Israel will become fantastically wealthy
4. the U.S. will lose its position of leadership
5. the U.S. will experience internal political chaos while Communist subversion erodes the economy
6. Increased unification of Western Europe
7. increased financial strength of Western Europe
8. increases in: a. crime b. riots c. lack of employment d. poverty
9. e. illiteracy f. mental illness g. illegitimacy and h. drug addiction
10. the merger of drugs and religion

To some extent the first two of these are subjective, but it appears to me that Christian churches are closer to the Bible today than they were in 1970. In the U.S., about 77 million Americans belonged to evangelical denominations in 1998[1] up from only 51 million in 1970. Born-again is now the

1. *LA Times* 6/21/98, A37.

mainstream of Protestantism. Roman Catholics have a Pope who says that every Christian must have the experience of reading the Gospels and meeting the person of Jesus Christ.[2] In June 1998, the Roman Catholic Church reversed the position it held for over 500 years, and now states that forgiveness and salvation come only by the Grace of God. It says that good works are only the result of Grace. While there is a grass-roots movement within the Roman Catholic Church to declare Mary as the co-redeemer of our sins with Jesus, this heresy has not been accepted by the Vatican.

Some mainline Protestant churches have moved away from the Bible since Lindsay's book was written, particularly on the issue of accepting homosexual practices and marriage. To some extent, this is only the continuation of a process which was begun centuries ago, but this process of liberalization is a principal reason why people have left mainline churches for "born-again" churches. In order for Lindsey's predictions to have any meaning, mainline churches would have to be moving away from the Bible at a faster rate than they were moving away in previous decades, and it is not apparent that this is the case. I believe that "born-again" Christians are more accepted by mainline denominations today than there were in 1970, and we are not persecuted by those churches. Due to the subjective nature of these predictions and the ambiguity of recent church history, I leave it to the reader to decide if these predictions are truer today than they were in 1970 or in 1980.

Israel is not fantastically wealthy. In fact, its per capita income in 1997 was about the same as Spain's, near the bottom of Western European nations.

The U.S. position of leadership (both economically and militarily) is at its strongest point since the end of World War II. We have fewer riots than in the 1960's and early 1970's. Our economy in recent years has been the most successful of any major nation. At this writing, unemployment in the U.S. is at a 28 year low, and our federal budget is expected to show a surplus in 1998. The dollar is the most widely accepted currency in the world.

Unification of Western Europe has been taking place since the time of Napoleon. (Unification was part of why Napoleon was believed by many of his contemporaries to be the Antichrist.) It is continuing, and, while Lindsey's biblical interpretations are based on a confederacy of ten European nations, currently fifteen nations are full members of the European Union. Eleven of those nations are part of the European Monetary Union.

---

2 Pope John Paul II *The Way to* Christ (New York: HarperOne, 1994) 16.

Preparation for the End Times

Another seventy nations outside of Europe are affiliated under the Lome Convention. European economies, however, have failed to perform as well as expected, and unemployment in much of Europe is at the highest levels in a half century.

Of the eight sociological variables which Lindsey expected to increase in the U.S., seven have decreased since 1980, and most have shown a net decrease since 1970. While drug use among teenagers increased from 1996 to 1998, the 1998 rate is still only half of the 1979 rate. The only variable which has increased since 1980 is the rate of illegitimacy, and even that variable depends on how the statistics are measured. Over the past two decades, the U.S. has had a decrease in the birth rate along with growth in the number of unwed women. Hence, if we define the illegitimacy rate as the number of illegitimate births divided by the total number of births, then the illegitimacy rate is rising, partially due to the fact that the denominator is falling. Alternatively, if we define the illegitimacy rate as the percentage of all unwed women of child-bearing age who give birth, then the illegitimacy rate is falling, partially due to the denominator rising. In 1997 the percentage of all unwed black women who gave birth to illegitimate children was at its lowest level since 1969.

I am not aware of any new associations of religion with drugs. I believe that this relationship reached its peak around the time of Lindsey's writing in 1970, and has decreased since then.

Other facts further erode Lindsey's theory. The USSR has dissolved and its largest former republic (Russia) is no longer a military power with the same rank as the United States. At the close of the Twentieth century, oil is cheaper relative to other goods than it was at any time in recorded history, and, as a consequence, the economic power of the Middle East has greatly diminished. Iran is courting a renewal of diplomatic relationships with the US.

There is a simple explanation for the cycle of the last thirty years. The U.S. faltered militarily, economically, and morally as a result of the Vietnam War. When President Nixon tried to correct the economy through a program of wage and price controls, taking the dollar off of the gold standard, and increasing import duties, the economy went further downhill. Nixon's illegal spying and subsequent resignation, cemented the moral decline. President Carter's policies continued the U.S.'s downhill slide which was finally reversed with the Reagan Revolution. As already noted, a born-again Christian in politics is a fish out of water, and the back-to back elections of evangelical Christians, Nixon and Carter, to the U.S. presidency apparently contributed to the conditions which made Lindsey's predictions seem true.

It must be said of Lindsay that his book played a role in leading many people to Christ, and that is certainly good. While Lindsay states that his forecasts are not infallible revelations from God, but only his own beliefs of what will happen, the fact that they failed to take place and were then changed in subsequent editions should make the reader leery of imputing any power to his model of biblical prophecy.

Despite the failure of Lindsey's predictions to be realized, many Christians continue to believe that Christ's return will be in the current generation. There are at least five possible biblical bases for this belief:

1. earthquakes and famines
2. the observation of particularly high selfishness and immorality today
3. a count of years either from the time of Daniel or since the Creation and the time of Christ
4. the worldwide preaching of the Gospel
5. the rebirth of the nation of Israel.

I. Earthquakes and Famines

The rate at which reported earthquakes take place has risen throughout the Twentieth century. This is a reporting phenomenon, however, and not a geological phenomenon. Seismic equipment is continually improving, and, as a consequence, there are many small earthquakes in remote parts of the world which are now detected. The growth in the number of reported earthquakes consists almost entirely of small earthquakes which would previously have been unnoticed or unconfirmed. The growth in deaths from earthquakes is simply due to the world having a larger population.

If we look only at very large earthquakes, those which are certain to be reported in any time period, then the rate at which earthquakes take place has fallen during the Twentieth century. In the first decade of the twentieth century there were four recorded earthquakes of a magnitude 8.0 or greater on the Richter scale. Four earthquakes of this magnitude took place in the 1970s, but only one took place in the 1980s, and none has taken place to date in the 1990s. There is certainly no pattern of great earthquakes taking place more frequently, and small earthquakes were mostly unrecorded until very recent times. Some Christians have arranged statistics on earthquakes in such a way as to show that they are increasing but, if an increase in earthquakes were a sign from God, I would expect the change to be apparent as opposed to an unobvious statistic.

The late Twentieth century has seen some of the world's worst famines, primarily in Africa. As already mentioned, the famines in Africa had political roots. It is sometimes the case that the group of Africans who control politics in a given country want the competing groups to die so that they can no longer compete. In Africa, starvation is used as a political tool. (Newsweek July 27, 1998 p. 13) While famine of this sort seems to fit the model of conditions preceding the Second Coming, these famines have been concentrated in Africa, and the rates of starvation throughout the rest of the world have been falling. Partially as a result of the success of the "Green Revolution," the world produces more food than ever before, and the overall rate at which the world's population has died from starvation has been declining.

II. High Selfishness and Immorality Today

Matthew 24:38 compares the last days on earth with the days of Noah, and some Christians interpret this to mean that those last days will be signaled by the lawless behavior of Noah's times (Genesis 6:1–5), although this interpretation is speculative. Most likely, Jesus is just saying that the coming of the Last Days will be a surprise to most people just as the Great Flood was a surprise. A clearer case for human corruption in the last days is in 2 Timothy 3:1–7 which describes selfish lovers of pleasure in the last days. Similarly, Matthew 24:12 says "And because lawlessness is increased, most people's love will grow cold."

In order for lawlessness and selfishness to indicate that we are currently in the last days, it would at least require that the degree of lawlessness and selfishness in the present age greatly exceeds that of past ages. Since ancient times people have decried the immorality of their own generation and longed for the honorable living which they believed existed in the past, and to a large extent, the people who believe that their fellow citizens are worse today than people of previous generations are simply comparing current reality with a past which has been fictitiously idealized.

Statistics on crime provide some evidence concerning whether the current generation is more selfish and lawless than past generations. Before presenting these statistics, the issue of accuracy must be addressed. Crime statistics are all based on reported crime. Just as recorded earthquakes vary from actual earthquakes, reported crime may be very different from actual crime. Victims may choose to not report crime out of fear, embarrassment, or the belief that reporting will do no good. When I was a student at the University of Chicago in the 1970s, I read that the burglary rate in Chicago was lower than the burglary rate in my hometown, Peoria, Illinois. I was very surprised by this until I had an incident in which my own automobile was vandalized in Chicago. When I went to a police station to report it, the officers were surprised that I even bothered to report the incident and somewhat suspicious that maybe I did it to create an insurance claim. They clearly intended to do nothing about it. When my parents experienced a similar incident in Peoria, the police took the report and, after some investigation around the city, actually caught the culprit who then made restitution. With these results, no one should be surprised that the rate of reported crime in Chicago was lower than the rate of reported crime in Peoria, since the victim in Chicago had comparatively little incentive to ever report crimes to the police. These differences across times and across regions may create statistics on reported crime which have little correlation to the actual rates at which crime takes place.

Statistics on homicide generally have the greatest accuracy because homicide is such a significant crime that it is unlikely to go unreported. In the U.S., we have statistics on the number and rates of major reported crimes in cities with populations greater than 25,000 from 1937 to the present. The number of murders and non-negligent homicides was 2,479 in 1937 or about 7.88 per 100,000 inhabitants of cities. In 1980 cities reported 23,040 murders and non-negligent homicides, but the population of U.S. cities with more than 25,000 inhabitants had also increased so that the rate was 10.2 per 100,000 inhabitants. In 1996, the total of murders and non-negligent homicides was 19,650, and the increased urban population meant that the rate was only 7.4 per 100,000 inhabitants. In other words, the most recent statistics on murder and non-negligent homicide in urban areas of the U.S. show a lower rate than in 1937, the first year for which those statistics are available.

The statistics for robbery are a little less reliable due to the fact that some robberies may not be reported. The rate at which robberies are reported is probably influenced by the expectation of how police will act, and whether or not the victims have insurance which requires reporting. The

Preparation for the End Times

rate of reported robberies per populations of 100,000 in cities in the U.S. has gone from 84.9 in 1937 to 258.7 in 1980 and 202.4 in 1996.

The statistics on violent crime in the U.S. also show that some important crimes have fallen dramatically. At the beginning of the century more than 100 black Americans were lynched each year. There have been no reported lynchings since the late 1950s. Other hate motivated crimes against minority races continue, but I suspect that they are less frequent than in the first half of the century.

Statistics on rates of crime are at odds with public perceptions. From 1990 to 1997 the total number of incidents of violent crime which were reported in the U.S. fell from 1.84 million to 1.59 million. Over the same period, the percentage of the public which tells pollsters that violent crime is their main worry has risen more than four fold. Part of the explanation for this may lie with the fact that the number of crime stories reported on national television networks has steadily risen since 1990, going from 757 stories reported in 1990 to 1,817 stories reported in 1997 (LA Times August 23, 1998).

Overall, the change in the rates of violent crime in the U.S. over the past sixty years is not clear. It may be rising, but this may simply be part of a cycle or an aberration of statistics. It may partially be the result of public desire to convict innocent people less frequently, with the consequence that the guilty are set free more frequently. Reduced rates of punishment have been shown to result in higher crime rates. The next few years should give us valuable evidence of whether or not violent crime in the U.S. is on a long-term upward trend. The current trend is that most violent crime rates are falling, and, if this continues, then I think that we are forced to conclude that the crime rate is not evidence of Christ's Second Coming.

Family relationships are another area where we may have evidence of increasing selfishness and coldness of hearts. They are also an area of lawlessness, since Jesus was probably talking about His Father's laws which include the laws of marriage. Divorce rates grew dramatically in this century, and, like abortion rates, peaked around 1980 and have since subsided to the lowest rates in over twenty years. More people are choosing to have children without marriage, and in the late 1990's approximately 30 percent of all births in the U.S. are to unmarried women. As noted in the chapter on behavior, lack of regard for the institution of marriage is a principal force behind these and other statistics indicating social decline.

Family relationships in the U.S. were altered by the so-called "sexual revolution" of the 1960's. As a result of effective birth control pills, the threat of pregnancy, an important deterrent to pre-marital sex, was reduced. The increased incidence of pre-marital sex (a form of lawlessness) has probably produced colder hearts among the current generation of young people. It is probably the best evidence that this is a generation of selfish lovers of pleasure. Like abortion and divorce, however, pre-marital sex is waning. Explaining an 11.9 percent decline in the birthrate for teenagers between 1991 and 1996 *Newsweek* states : "Teens are simply choosing to not have sex . . . an indication that the once ridiculed idea of advocating abstinence may be catching on." The same article quotes Isabel Sawhill, President of the National Campaign to Prevent Teen Pregnancy, "We seem to have succeeded in convincing teens that delaying sex may be a better idea, because more are doing it." The article also notes that "teens consistently report that they wish their parents would give them specific advice on dating, sexually transmitted diseases and how to say no to sex." The latest statistics indicate that the teen age birthrate continued to decline in 1997, and abstinence from pre-marital sex is cited as the primary reason for the decline.

Even if the condition of lawlessness gives some evidence of being fulfilled, it does not appear that the evidence is strong. Declines in rates of abortion, murder, divorce and pre-marital sex over the last ten years mean that it is difficult to make a case for a general increase in lawlessness. While some lawlessness has increased in recent years (such as drug use among teenagers) at its worst, the evidence concerning overall lawlessness is statistically ambiguous. I do not believe, however, that the fulfillment of biblical prophecies concerning the Second Coming will be ambiguous.

III. The Count of Years in the Bible

The count of years from the time of Daniel was the principal source of the prediction of the Second Coming by William Miller, a leader in the Second Adventist movement. It is also used by Jehovah's Witnesses whose movement was probably influenced by the Second Adventists' predictions. These believers have interpreted Daniel's prophetic interpretation of King Nebuchadnezzar's dream (Daniel 4) to mean that the time from the Jewish captivity in Babylon until the end times would be a number of years equal to seven times the number of days in a year. Using a lunar year of 360 days, this is 2,520 years. William Miller' count of years took him to 1844. Charles

Preparation for the End Times

Taze Russell, the founder of the Jehovah's Witnesses, began the count with Jerusalem's destruction in approximately 607 B.C. The addition of 2,520 years took him to 1913. Later counts by Jehovah's Witnesses began with the return of the Jews to Jerusalem in approximately 537 BC, and 2,520 years added to that takes us to 1983. If we use Russell's start date, and a 365 day solar year instead of the 360 day lunar year, we wind up at 1948, a close approximation of the 1948 re-birth of Israel. If we start with the date of the return of the Jews to Jerusalem, we wind up with 2018, a few years from this writing.

Another count of years is made from the time of creation in the book of Genesis. Based on the ages of patriarchs and various events reported in the Old Testament, creation took place in approximately 4000 BC. The year cannot be determined with exactness due to uncertainty about some of the dates after the Babylonian exile, but most estimates are very close to 4000 BC. James Ussher, the Anglican Archbishop of Ireland in the mid-1600's, calculated creation to have taken place in 4004 BC at noon on October 23, but such a calculation obviously required many historical and theological assumptions.[3*]

Using the analogy that a day for the Lord is a thousand years for man, there were four days before Christ's birth, and two more days will have passed by the year 2000. (Of course, the pivotal event for Christianity was the crucifixion in 33 AD, rather than Christ's birth.) Those six days represent the six working days of the week, to be followed by a one day Sabbath for the Lord, the one thousand year reign of Christ. This theory states that Christ's return will be near to the year 2000 (or 2033 based on the crucifixion.)

There are at least two problems with the determination of Christ's Second Coming by counts of years. First, the biblical bases for these counts are unclear. The Bible does not instruct us to determine the time of the Second Coming in either of these manners. Alternative interpretations are just as likely.

A second problem with these predictions is that the date of the Second Coming is known only by the Father. Jesus Christ Himself stated that it

---

3. One of the assumptions required for this count of years since Creation is that Adam was the first man and was therefore created on the Sixth Day. While the idea that Adam was the first man is a reasonable inference and is part of tradition, it is not explicitly stated in the Bible. The only statement of Adam as the first man is 1Cor 15:45 in which it refers to Adam as the first man and Jesus Christ as the second man. Clearly, this does not indicate that Adam was created first.

was known by no man, not even himself. While Jesus did not share the full knowledge of his Father's mind, he clearly understood Scriptures better than any mortal can even imagine! Jesus could, therefore, have made either of these counts of years with perfect precision, and determined the year (if not the actual day) in which he would return. He was obviously unable to do this. I therefore believe that it is arrogant for a mortal mind to even attempt to determine the time of Christ's Second Coming using only Scriptures and dates which were known to Jesus Christ.

IV. Worldwide Preaching of the Gospel

In Matthew 24:14 Jesus states "And this Gospel of the kingdom shall be preached in the whole world for a witness to all nations, and then the end shall come." Of the five possible reasons for believing that we are currently in the last days, this is the one with the clearest biblical authority. It is only a question of detail as to whether this condition has been fulfilled. Nineteenth century millenarian Christians believed that the Gospel had been preached in every nation of the world by the early 1800's, and it confirmed their other reasons for believing that they were in end times. In the late twentieth century, however, missionaries are still finding new tribes and places where the gospel has not been heard. Since these places are becoming fewer and smaller every year, we must be very close to meeting the condition that the gospel has been preached to the entire world.

The preaching of the gospel to the entire world is only a condition which will take place before the end. The idea that the end will come immediately after this condition has been fulfilled is an easily drawn inference, but it is not a necessary implication. It would not be inconsistent with Scriptures if there were a wait of some years or even centuries between the preaching of the gospel to the whole world and Christ's second coming.

V. Israel

The fifth reason for believing that Christ's Second Coming is imminent is the rebirth of Israel. Chapters 34–37 of Ezekiel prophesies the return of Jacob's descendants to the land of Israel. It says that the Lord's people will be gathered from many nations and Israel and Judah will become one again. Chapter 38 says that (vs. 1)"Gog of the land of Magog, the prince of Rosh (possibly Russia), Meshach, and Tubal" will (v. 8) "in the latter years come

Preparation for the End Times

into the land that is restored from the sword" probably meaning Israel. The belief, based on Ezekiel, that we are in the Last Days is derived from the words "in the latter years" in Ezekiel 38:8.

The problem with this interpretation is fairly obvious: neither Russia nor any other nation has invaded Israel. If such an invasion takes place, it could well be an indication that we are in the Last Days. In no place does Ezekiel say that rebirth of the nation-state of Israel would be a sign of the last days. If Ezekiel's "land that is restored from the sword" is the State of Israel, then it may imply that Israel's rebirth was a necessary condition for the Last Days to take place. It is not, however, a sufficient condition on its own.

It is also worthy of note that Judah and Israel have not become one. As I described in the chapter on Israel, Jews are all descendants of the tribes of Levi, Judah, and Benjamin while the house of Israel includes some Levites as well as all of the descendants of the other nine tribes. The Bible tells us that those other nine tribes were taken into Assyria and are still there. No reconciliation or return has taken place. Christians who seek to bring about the conditions for the last days should want to bring peace in the Middle East, thereby enabling reconciliation of the houses of Judah and Israel.

The second set of verses indicating that Israel's rebirth may be a sign of the end times is the parable of the fig tree. Matthew 24:32–34 tells us "Now learn the parable from the fig tree: when its branch has already become tender, and puts forth its leaves, you know that summer is near; even so you too, when you see all of these things, recognize that he is near, right at the door. Truly I say to you, this generation will not pass away until all these things take place."

Previously, in Matthew 21:18–22, Jesus had found a fig tree which had leaves but no fruit. he touched the tree and said "No longer shall there ever be any fruit from you." At once the tree withered. Many Christians believe that this fig tree represented Israel, and that seems a likely interpretation to me as well. Since Israel did not "bear fruit" by accepting Jesus as the Christ, it withered. As Jesus prophesied, Israel was invaded, and the Temple was destroyed. All of that took place by 72 AD, however, and that is consistent with the statement that "this generation will not pass away," meaning the generation of Jesus' disciples. In other words, the word "this" does not mean "that". This is the most obvious interpretation, especially since those events took place within 40 years of when Jesus predicted them. I regard Hank Hanegraaf (the Bible Answer Man on radio) as one of the best Bible interpreters who speak on the radio, and that is also Hanegraaf's interpretation.

Today numerous websites post harsh criticisms of Hanegraaf for making this interpretation, and it appears that this interpretation was the principle reason for a network of radio stations operated by Christian dispensationalists to have eliminated the Bible Answer Man program and replaced it with a similar question and answer program which I find to generally be less biblically accurate.

Israel's rebirth is an historical phenomenon without precedent. While Jews were already scattered throughout the world before 70 AD,[8] after the destruction of the Temple they dispersed further. For 1878 years the Jews had no homeland, yet somehow they retained their identity. I know of no other ethnic group that has retained its identity under similar circumstances. Even Gypsies were not as scattered or as long without a homeland as the Jews.

It is even more amazing that these scattered people would somehow reclaim their Promised Land and form the State of Israel. To some extent, millennial Christians played a role in Israel's rebirth, so there is an aspect of this only being a self-fulfilling prophecy (see chapter on Israel). Even then, this was a very unusual event in world history, and it is not surprising that most believers who have looked at these events have said that it is evidence of the Hand of God.

Whether or not this is fulfillment of the prophecy in Matthew 24 is another question. The 31 verses preceding Matthew 24:32 deal with the events of the end times, and are mostly Jesus' answer to the disciples' question "When will these things be, and what will be the sign of your coming and the end of the age." The most straightforward interpretation to verse 33 "…when you see all of these things…" is that "these things" are the events of the previous 25 verses, and, just as we know that summer is near when we see the leaves on a fig tree, so we will know that Christ's return is imminent when we see the events of verses 5–31.

We are not told that the fig tree is Israel. While a fig tree probably represents Israel in Matthew 21, and possibly also in Song of Solomon 2:13, it has many other uses throughout the Bible. Most of the uses of "fig tree" in the Bible are just to fig trees. The fig tree is also used for other representations as in Judges 9:10–15. More pertinent, in Luke 21:5 the apostles again ask, "Teacher, when therefore will these things be? And what will be the sign when these things are about to take place?" In response (Luke 21:29), Jesus describes events similar to those in Matthew 24 and provides the same parable, saying "Behold the fig trees and all of the trees." This indicates that

Preparation for the End Times

He is referring to the property held by all deciduous trees that they put forth leaves before the summer. Just as their leaves are harbingers of the summer, so the events described in the preceding verses will be harbingers of the Lord's coming. Those events of the previous verses, however, do not include the rebirth of Israel.

I find it difficult to believe that the formation of a secular state constitutes an allegorical budding of a fig tree. Another interpretation of the budding of the fig tree is that it is the outpouring of the Holy Spirit on contemporary Christians. I have personally witnessed the Holy Spirit in my own life, and this may be happening to a growing number of Christians. It would be difficult to assert, however, that the outpourings of the Holy Spirit in the late twentieth century were so much greater than those of the many previous Christian revivals that this constitutes the singular sign of a budding of the fig tree while the others did not.

Lindsey noted that many theologians considered a biblical generation to be forty years, but at this writing fifty years have passed since Israel's rebirth. Seventy years represents a person's life span in Psalms 90:10, and that time added to Israel's year of birth puts the Second Coming at 2018. The generation which was alive in 1948 will probably not pass away, however, until at least 2070. As already noted, longevity is increasing, so some people who were born prior to 1948 may still be living even in the Twenty-second century.

Prophecy on the Second Coming refers to the abomination of desolation which is the desecration of the Temple. The general interpretation of this prophecy is that the Temple refers to the building in which Jews held their daily sacrifices. If that is so, the Temple must be rebuilt, possibly, but not necessarily on its former site at the Temple Mount in Jerusalem. This is currently the site of the Dome of the Rock, the second holiest shrine of Islam. Construction on that site virtually requires that a government of religious Jews rules Jerusalem. Furthermore, construction on this site would almost certainly incite an Islamic Holy War against Israel which could be further fulfillment of biblical prophecy. It is also possible that the abomination of Desolation was something else altogether. As noted in my chapter on the Economics of Politics, it was not the first desire of the Lord that the Temple should be built. Furthermore, Jesus repeatedly referred to the His Body as the Temple, and that would lead to the abomination of desolation not being something involving a building made of wood and stone.

Luke 21: 24 presents another possible indication that we are in the End Times. In this verse Jesus is apparently describing the destruction of Jerusalem (68–70AD) and states, "Jerusalem will be trampled under the foot of the Gentiles until the times of the Gentiles be fulfilled." Since Jerusalem is now ruled by Jews, it appears that the time of the Gentiles has been fulfilled. It is not clear, however, whether Luke 24:28–32 is referring back to verse 24 when the parable of the fig tree is presented and we are told (vs. 31) "Even so you, too, when you see these things happening, recognize that the Kingdom of God is near." Alternatively, verse 31 may only be referring to the astronomical and geophysical signs in verse 25.

A possible flaw with all of the theories stating that Israel's rebirth portends the Second Coming is the fact that the Lord's coming will be as much a surprise as the arrival of a thief in the night. It is a surprise which faithful Christians have prepared for throughout the centuries with no political signs that it was coming. They had no particular reason to believe that theirs was the generation in which the Second Coming would take place, but relied on Christ's words that they must always be prepared.

It is disappointing to see that many of the most dedicated Christians today believe that political signs indicate that Christ's Second Coming will be in their own generation. The reason for my disappointment is that simple analysis suggests that these Christians would not be so dedicated without their belief in Christ's imminent return. These Christians sometimes expect rewards on earth in short order for their dedication.

My disappointment is that, to the extent the Imminent Pre-millennial Christians have become dedicated due to this belief, they may have lacked dedication without this belief. Christ is concerned with our hearts, and behavior is secondary. The beliefs of the Imminent Pre-millennialists may be grounded in sandy soil. Since 1980 there has been little, if any, new evidence that Christ's return is imminent, and some of the old evidence has been reversed. When Christ did not return in 1844, the non-event was called "The Great Disappointment" by the Millerites. Many assemblies broke up as a consequence. Christians who spoke of the Second Coming lost credibility as a result of the false prediction. Similarly, there is a loss in membership of the Jehovah's Witnesses every time a prophecy fails to be realized. An evangelical preacher was recently quoted as saying that if it were not for the existence of the nation of Israel, he did not know if he would continue to believe in God.[4] Because of these possibilities, Christians must be very

4. Hefley, 1978.

Preparation for the End Times

careful when they interpret current events to mean that Christ's return is imminent. A false prediction could destroy the faith of believers and create a barrier which stops the unsaved from ever seeking the Lord. A false prediction may also make it more difficult for people to believe that Christ's return is imminent when genuine signs appear.

Christians must also be careful when their behavior is motivated by the belief that current events indicate the Lord's Second Coming. This may require fine discernment. Throughout the centuries, all Christians have known that the Lord is coming and that His return could take place at any time. We must therefore be prepared, and even though we are in this world, we are not of this world. We are only strangers who are passing through.

We need, however, to consider our legacy to those who remain in this world. The belief that we are in the End Times has sometimes prompted Christians into extreme acts which have made them poor examples. Thomas Muntzer's Millenarian beliefs were partially responsible for the Thuringian revolt of 1525, bringing death to Muntzer and other Anabaptists. In 1857 the African tribe of Xhosa combined the Millenarian message of missionaries with tribal beliefs to produce a religious fervor in which they killed many of their cattle. About a third of the tribe subsequently died of starvation. In 1915 the millenarian, John Chilembwe, a graduate of an American theological seminary, lead a revolt in African Nyasaland (now Malawi). Chilembwe and many of his followers were killed. Millenarian beliefs combined with incorrect biblical interpretations to lead thirty-nine members of the Heaven's Gate cult to commit suicide in March 1997.

While it is easy to understand that violent or cult-oriented responses to the Millennial message have made bad examples of its adherents, conventional Christian Millenarian views have also led to behavior which made us poor witnesses. James Watt, Secretary of the Interior under Ronald Reagan, was a Millenarian and a member of Pentecostal Assembly of God. While in office he acquired notoriety for his statement that we need not invest the government's time and money in preventing environmental deterioration since the Second Coming would take place before much damage could be done.

The problem with all of these examples was that Christians imposed costs on other people as a result of their beliefs in the imminence of Christ's Second Coming. Even though their behavior was partially motivated by their belief in Christ's imminent return, their behavior was not Christian behavior. The imminence of the Lord's Return is not a reason for Christians to sanction the despoiling of natural resources. Despoiling of the environment can actually be one of the signs preceding a period of Tribulation, and Christians who participate in this are not making themselves good witnesses. This is especially true since the despoiling would take place so that private businesses could produce more material wealth in the interim. This is not a particularly Christian goal whether the Lord's return is imminent or in the distant future.

Active Dispensationalism

One of the greatest dangers associated with Christian participation in politics is active dispensationalism. Dispensationalism for Christians is the belief that God has made separate promises to different groups of people. Consequently, most dispensationalists believe that lands in the Middle East were promised to modern Jews and that Jews have special blessings which are not available to Gentiles (see chapter on Israel for further explanation). Some dispensationalists also believe that some messages from Jesus (like the Sermon on the Mount) are not intended for Christians to follow until Christ's return. Modern dispensationalism began around 1870 with the teachings of John Darby who said that the world would worsen, Israel would again become a nation in the land of Palestine, the Antichrist would rise, and then Christ would return for His Church prior to the Great Tribulation. These teachings were continued with the writing and ministry of C.I. Scofield in the U.S., and many of Hal Lindsay's prophecies concerning Israel are taken from Scofield.

I am using the term "active dispensationalism" to indicate the belief that Christians are called to consciously act in a manner which brings about the prophecies of the Bible, even when we are not otherwise called on to behave in this manner. I believe that active dispensationalism is possibly the most spiritually dangerous temptation which born-again Christians face today.

Christians are clearly called to bring about the fulfillment of some prophecies. Jesus prophesied "And this gospel of the kingdom shall be preached in the whole world for a witness to the nations, and then the end shall come."(Mt 24:14) After His resurrection, Jesus told his disciples "Go therefore and make disciples of all nations, baptizing them in the name of the Father and the Son and the Holy Spirit, teaching them to observe all that I commanded you . . ." (Mt 28:19–20) Clearly from this we know that Christians should consciously act in a way which will fulfill Jesus' prophecy about the preaching of the gospel before end times will come. As I have already suggested in this chapter, working to bring about reconciliation between the houses of Judah and Israel would also be in keeping with Christian behavior since Jesus told us that peacemakers are blessed.

There are other prophecies concerning end times which Christians should clearly not fulfill. For example, much of the book of Revelations deals with the failures of the church and the wicked deeds of political leaders. It tells us that Christians will be persecuted and martyred. Clearly, we do not want to act in a way which brings those wicked events about, and I know of no Christians who say that we should.

The dangerous areas are in parts of prophecy which do not seem wicked and which are to take place before the Second Coming. The temptation is to try to bring those prophetic events to immediate fruition to pave the way (so to speak) for Christ's return. Except for specific behaviors such as witnessing and making peace, however, we are not told to pave the way for Christ's return. Our Heavenly Father knows the day and hour when the return will take place, and no conscious act on our parts can change that day or hour.

Some Christians have armed themselves in preparation for participation in Armageddon. Other Christians are reluctant to support peace in the Middle East since they believe that a great war in the Middle East would be the fulfillment of prophecy. This behavior is harmful to Christ's cause. It involves Christians committing acts which are unChristian. Through those acts, they make themselves bad examples and make it more difficult for other people to be saved.

It is the will of the Lord that all should be saved. Satan wants to prevent this. About twenty percent of the world's people are Muslims, so it is important that Christians make themselves good witnesses for those people. Even if Armageddon will take place in the Middle East very soon, we should try to witness to Muslims and not harden their hearts. This is our command from Christ.

We do not know the Lord's plan as to when Armageddon will take place, and nothing that we can do will stop the Lord's plan. If we act peacefully to win new souls for Christ, then we have not gone against God's will, but only served as Christ's faithful servants. Alternatively, if we act violently under a false belief that Armageddon is here, then we have been seduced by Satan. Our own souls will be damaged as we realize the disgrace that we have brought on the Christian name. The souls of other people will be damaged as well. It is difficult for an unbeliever to forgive a Christian who has participated in killing the unbeliever's family members. That difficulty may be a barrier to receiving Christ.

Some of the dispensational circumstances for Christ's return, such as the existence of the State of Israel and the existence of a physical building on the site of the former Temple of Solomon are inferences which are not necessarily implied from Scriptures. Millennial Christians played at least a small role in the creation of the State of Israel, and their role is increasing through their influence on U.S. foreign policy.

We know that the Lord is coming soon because He has told us. There is a possibility that computer chips implanted in the forehead or forearm will be the Mark of the Beast, so I would not agree to this procedure. Nonetheless, many Christians throughout history have been mistaken in their belief in the imminence of the Lord's Second Coming, so contemporary Christians must be careful with our behavior. Until we witness clear and incontestable signs such as the sun darkened and the moon not giving its light, (Mt 24:29) we must take care that we do not act in a way such that if the Lord does not return when we expect that we have made ourselves poor witnesses for Christ.

Conclusion

CHRISTIANITY IS A SPIRITUAL movement based on a relationship with God through our Savior, Jesus Christ. This relationship changes the souls of people so that they are born-again, and their behavior changes as part of the process of sanctification. Christians are called to know God better and to allow the Holy Spirit to sanctify their lives. As this takes place, the old self dies, and a new person is born.

Early Christians influenced politics only through their prayer, charity, witnessing, and good behavior. The world opposed them. They were persecuted, although only a small number actually died as martyrs, and most of those martyrs died knowing that they could save their lives simply by throwing incense on the Roman Emperor's statue. Despite persecution, Christianity prospered, growing from a few thousand souls in 33 AD to probably more than half of the Roman Empire in 311 AD. The emperors of Rome gave up fighting Christianity, and persecution ended in 311 AD. The Emperor Constantine said that he converted to Christianity in 312, although he waited over a decade to state this publicly.

Christianity probably reached its early apex in 311 AD. More than half of the people in the Mediterranean world were Christian by that date, despite the fact that Christianity was illegal. The Christians at that time clearly had a strong spiritual commitment. At that time, it was unlikely that anyone would have said that he was a Christian simply because it was easier or because everyone else was a Christian. By contrast, after Constantine's acceptance of Christianity, it was easier for someone to say that he was Christian, even if he lacked a relationship with God through Jesus Christ. I therefore find it difficult to believe that everyone who professed the Christian faith after the fourth century actually knew Jesus Christ.

Constantine's acceptance of Christianity was the beginning of Christianity's relationship with the state. That relationship became a seduction in that it took Christians away from their relationship with God. The relationship took place under the guise that the state was protecting Christianity,

Conclusion

despite the fact that Christianity had survived and thrived without the protection of the state. The reality was that the state sought legitimacy through its association with Christianity. The state is always a fragile entity, and Christianity's association with the state meant that some people lost faith when the state failed. Muslims conquered the Southern and Eastern portions of the Mediterranean region, and by the year 800 most of the people in those countries had voluntarily converted to Islam. Many of the Europeans who did not convert to Islam only understood Christianity as a religious institution which preserved the power of their worldly king. People began to think of nations as being "Christian nations," ignoring the fact that the acceptance of Christ is a decision which must be separately made by each individual. The relationships which are produced by those individual decisions are so important that the Heavenly Father sent His Only Begotten Son, Jesus Christ to die for them. We are the Bride of Christ, but when believers have pledged allegiance to the state instead of to Christ, they have been seduced. This seduction has persisted until the Modern Age, and it may be the greatest spiritual loss since the date when Adam and Eve succumbed to sin in the Garden of Eden.

The late twentieth century has seen a re-birth of people having a personal relationship with the Lord. In the United States, the majority of Protestants say that they are born again. The Roman Catholic Church has officially taken the position that people are saved by grace and not by works. The Gospel is being preached in virtually every nation of the world, and there is real hope that we will resume and surpass the level of belief which prevailed in 311 AD.

Along with this hope there is also the fear of new seduction. In the United States several political organizations have given themselves Christian names, and they are urging believers to join them. Many Christians have responded to their call. The Bible tells us that Christians will be known by their love for one another, but, among many Americans, Christians are known primarily by their political positions. All of those political positions involve the forcing of behavior or the transfer of property belonging to unbelievers. It makes the unbelievers think that, as the disciples falsely believed (Acts 1:6), the Kingdom of Christ is a worldly kingdom. The consequence to unbelievers has been a hardening of the hearts so that it is more difficult for them to receive the Gospel. The consequence to Christians has been a worldly alliance which takes them away from their spiritual relationship with the Lord.

The one important battle in world history has been the battle for the souls of men. It is the ultimate motivation for the pursuit of wealth since,

Conclusion

beyond the bare necessities of life, wealth is meaningless except for its ability to influence people. Sex, also, is not about physical pleasure; it is about souls, as are all personal relationships. The importance of the soul is the reason why all of the great wars of the twentieth century have taken place under the mask of ideology. Ideologies such as communism, fascism, and democracy can capture souls, and once the soul is captured the body follows.

When a person receives Jesus as Lord and Savior, Christ enters his soul. Jesus said "Abide in me, and I in you." and "he who abides in me and I in him, he bears much fruit, for apart from me you can do nothing. If anyone does not abide in me, he is thrown away as a branch and dries up." and "They gather them and cast them into the fire and they are burned." "If you abide in me and my words abide in you, ask whatever you wish, and it shall be done for you" (John 15:4–7). Jesus Christ wants our souls. The Christian who gives himself to Christ may have whatever he wants simply by asking, but the Christian who tries to create accomplishments apart from Christ can do nothing.

There is opposition to Christ in this battle. Satan also wants our souls. Because Satan is the Prince of this World, the world hates Christianity. "If you were of the world, the world would love its own; but because you are not of the world, but I chose you out of the world, therefore the world hates you" (John 15:19). As Christians who give our souls to Christ, we cannot be part of the world. We cannot use worldly methods, and we cannot make alliances with worldly people and causes. We must accept the hatred of the world and give love in return. Accepting hatred and responding with love would be an impossible task without the help of the Holy Spirit. When we yield to Christ, we have that help and can do anything.

Christians are the Bride of Christ, and we must prepare ourselves for the great apex of Christianity, Christ's Second Coming. The Groom has given us specific instructions for our behavior, and those instructions never tell us to participate in politics or to otherwise force unbelievers to behave better. Instead, they are instructions about love, worship, prayer, purity in our own behavior, and sharing the Good News of Christ's coming with others.

As the Bride of Christ, we look forward to the Great Wedding Feast which will take place with Christ's return. We cannot let our souls become occupied with any matter other than our Groom. We cannot let ourselves associate with causes or methods which are unholy. We cannot let ourselves be seduced.

Bibliography

Frend, W.H.C. *Martyrdom and Persecution in the Early Church.* Garden City, NY: Anchor Books Doubleday, 1967.

Hefley, James and Marti. *Arabs, Christians, and Jews.* Hannibal, MO:Hannibal Books, 1991.

Kramnick, Isaac, and R. Laurence Moore. *The GodlessConstitution.* New York: WW Norton, 1996.

McCullough, David. *Truman.* New York: Simon and Schuster, 1992.

Nietzsche, Friedrich. *Human, All Too Human.* (M. Faber and S. Lehmann, Trans.) Lincoln: University of Nebraska Press, 1984. Translated by Marion Faber with Stephen Lehmann.

Nietzsche, Friedrich. *Beyond Good and Evil.* (H. Zimmern, Trans.) New York: Russell and Russell, 1964.

Oldfield, Duane. *The Right and the Righteous.* Lanham, MD: Roman & Littlefield, 1996.

www.ingramcontent.com/pod-product-compliance
Lightning Source LLC
Chambersburg PA
CBHW051103160426
43193CB00010B/1299